DISEASES & DISORDERS

Amnesia

Titles in the Diseases and Disorders series include:

Acne
AIDS
Allergies
Alzheimer's Disease
Anorexia and Bulimia
Anthrax
Anxiety Disorders
Arthritis
Asthma
Attention Deficit Disorder
Autism
Bipolar Disorder
Birth Defects
Blindness
Breast Cancer
Cerebral Palsy
Childhood Obesity
Chronic Fatigue Syndrome
Cystic Fibrosis
Deafness
Dementia
Diabetes
Down Syndrome
Dyslexia
Epilepsy
Fetal Alcohol Syndrome
Food Poisoning
Growth Disorders
Headaches
Heart Disease
Hemophilia
Hepatitis
Hodgkin's Disease
Human Papillomavirus (HPV)
Leukemia
Lou Gehrig's Disease
Lyme Disease
Mad Cow Disease
Malaria
Malnutrition
Measles and Rubella
Meningitis
Mental Retardation
Mood Disorders
Multiple Sclerosis
Muscular Dystrophy
Obesity
Ovarian Cancer
Parkinson's Disease
Phobias
Prostate Cancer
SARS
Schizophrenia
Sexually Transmitted Diseases
Sleep Disorders
Smallpox
Strokes
Teen Depression
Toxic Shock Syndrome
Tuberculosis
West Nile Virus

DISEASES & DISORDERS

Amnesia

Jenny MacKay

LUCENT PRESS

Published in 2009 by
Lucent Press, an Imprint of Greenhaven Publishing, LLC
353 3rd Avenue
Suite 255
New York, NY 10010

LIBRARY OF CONGRESS CATALOGING-IN-PUBLICATION DATA

MacKay, Jenny, 1978-
Amnesia / by Jenny MacKay.
p. cm. — (Diseases and disorders)
Includes bibliographical references and index.
ISBN 978-1-4205-0040-0 (hardcover)
1. Amnesia—Juvenile literature. I. Title.
RC394.A5M33 2009
616.85'232—dc22

2008033757

CPSIA compliance information: Batch #BW09KL: For further information contact Greenhaven Publishing LLC, New York, New York, at 1-844-317-7404.

Please visit our website, www.greenhavenpublishing.com. For a free color catalog of all our high-quality books, call toll free 1-844-317-7404 or fax 1-844-317-7405.

Printed in the United States of America
1 2 3 4 5 6 7 13 12 11 10 09

Table of Contents

FOREWORD

"The Most Difficult Puzzles Ever Devised"

Charles Best, one of the pioneers in the search for a cure for diabetes, once explained what intrigued him so about medical research: "It's not just the gratification of knowing one is helping people," he confided, "although that probably is a more heroic and selfless motivation. Those feelings may enter in, but truly, what I find best is the feeling of going toe to toe with nature, of trying to solve the most difficult puzzles ever devised. The answers are there somewhere, those keys that will solve the puzzle and make the patient well. But how will those keys be found?"

Since the dawn of civilization, nothing has so puzzled people—and often frightened them, as well—as the onset of illness in a body or mind that seemed healthy before. Being unable to reverse conditions such as a seizure, the inability of a heart to pump, or the sudden deterioration of muscle tone in a small child, or even to understand why they occur was unspeakably frustrating to healers. Even before there were names for such conditions, before they were understood at all, each was a reminder of how complex the human body was and how vulnerable.

While our grappling with understanding diseases has been frustrating at times, it has also provided some of humankind's most heroic accomplishments. Alexander Fleming's accidental discovery in 1928 of a mold that could be turned into penicillin has resulted in the saving of untold millions of lives. The isolation of the enzyme insulin has reversed what was once a death sentence for anyone with diabetes. There also have been great strides in combating conditions for which there is not yet a cure. Medicines can help AIDS patients live longer, diagnostic tools such as mammography and ultrasounds can help doctors find tumors while they are treatable, and laser surgery techniques have made the most intricate, minute operations routine.

This "toe-to-toe" competition with diseases and disorders is even more remarkable when viewed in a historical continuum. An astonishing amount of progress has been made in a very short time. Just two hundred years ago, the existence of germs as a cause of some diseases was unknown. In fact, less than 150 years ago a British surgeon named Joseph Lister had difficulty persuading his fellow doctors that washing their hands before delivering a baby might increase the chances of a healthy delivery (especially if they had just attended to a diseased patient)!

Each book in Lucent's Diseases and Disorders series explores a disease or disorder and the knowledge that has been accumulated (or discarded) by doctors through the years. Each book also examines the tools used for pinpointing a diagnosis, as well as the various means that are used to treat or cure a disease. Finally, new ideas are presented—techniques or medicines that may be on the horizon.

Frustration and disappointment are still part of medicine because not every disease or condition can be cured or prevented. But the limitations of knowledge are constantly being pushed outward; the "most difficult puzzles ever devised" are finding challengers every day.

The Mystery of Memory Loss

A man wanders into a restaurant in a very small town. He recognizes nobody. He cannot name the special of the day, and he does not know the waitress who asks if he wants his usual. He looks around, confused, as people wave and say, "Hello, Jim." Everyone seems to know him, but he cannot remember any of them. He cannot remember his own last name. In fact, he has no memories. No memories at all.

When most people hear the word *amnesia*, they think of a situation like this: A person has lived through a serious accident or a very scary event, or simply wakes up one morning with no idea who he is, where he is from, or what he did the day before.

In reality, amnesia rarely affects people quite this way. Movies and television shows are to blame for a lot of the confusion. They make amnesia seem like something that happens often and to many people. A great many characters in soap operas, for example, suffer from severe amnesia for a while (some of them even have the condition more than once in their life). When they recover, their lost memories flood in. They remember all the people they have loved. It is a happy time for everyone, and life goes back to normal.

This is a far different story than most cases of real-life amnesia. Although the word *amnesia* means a loss of memory, most people who have the condition do not lose all of their past memories for just a short while, then suddenly get them back again and go on to live a normal life. Amnesia is much more unpredictable. It usually affects only part of a person's memory—the memory of many years or of just a few months or days or moments. The memory loss itself can last minutes or a lifetime.

Some amnesiacs may lose their memories about *how* to do things, too. A piano player might forget the notes to favorite songs she knew by heart, or she might forget how to read sheet music altogether. Other people "forget" how to make new memories. Amnesiacs might be able to remember things that happened to them long ago but not be able to remember anything new. Amnesia can also mean a loss of just a person's short-term memory, so that when a student's teacher tells him to take out his science book and turn to page ninety-six, he has already forgotten the page number by the time he finds the right book.

Amnesia can even work backwards, erasing the most recent memories first. This is what happens in Alzheimer's disease, a condition that causes a person to slowly lose his or her most recent memories. After a while, only the memories from childhood remain, as if all the years in between never happened at all.

Amnesia is not a disease, however. It is a condition that can be caused by diseases such as Alzheimer's. It can also be a result of a serious injury to the head, or it can be caused by drug or alcohol abuse. There are even cases of amnesia that seem to be caused by an upsetting event in a person's life. Whatever the origin, and however amnesia plays out for the person who has it, the loss of memories or of the ability to remember is something scientists are trying to better understand. Amnesia of any type is very complicated, because it happens in the brain—by far the most complex human organ, and the one that scientists know the least about.

Studies of the human brain, how it works, and how memories are made are helping scientists to better understand amnesia. New technology gives doctors and scientists the ability to take pictures of the brain and to draw electrical maps of what is working inside our skulls, and how, and when. Some psychologists and psychiatrists use methods such as hypnosis to try to help people with amnesia remember things that have been forgotten. Doctors are seeking ways to cure or prevent some of the diseases and conditions that can lead to memory loss in the first place.

Science may be getting closer to understanding amnesia, but the people who have it often lead very frustrating and difficult lives, and so do their families and friends. There may be little that anyone can do to find lost memories or remember how to learn again. There are so many types of amnesia and so many ways to lose memories that for most people, there is no cure. The happy endings we see in movies and soap operas do not always come for real-life people with amnesia. They may

A person with amnesia may lose the ability to recall past memories, or may be unable to form and retain new memories.

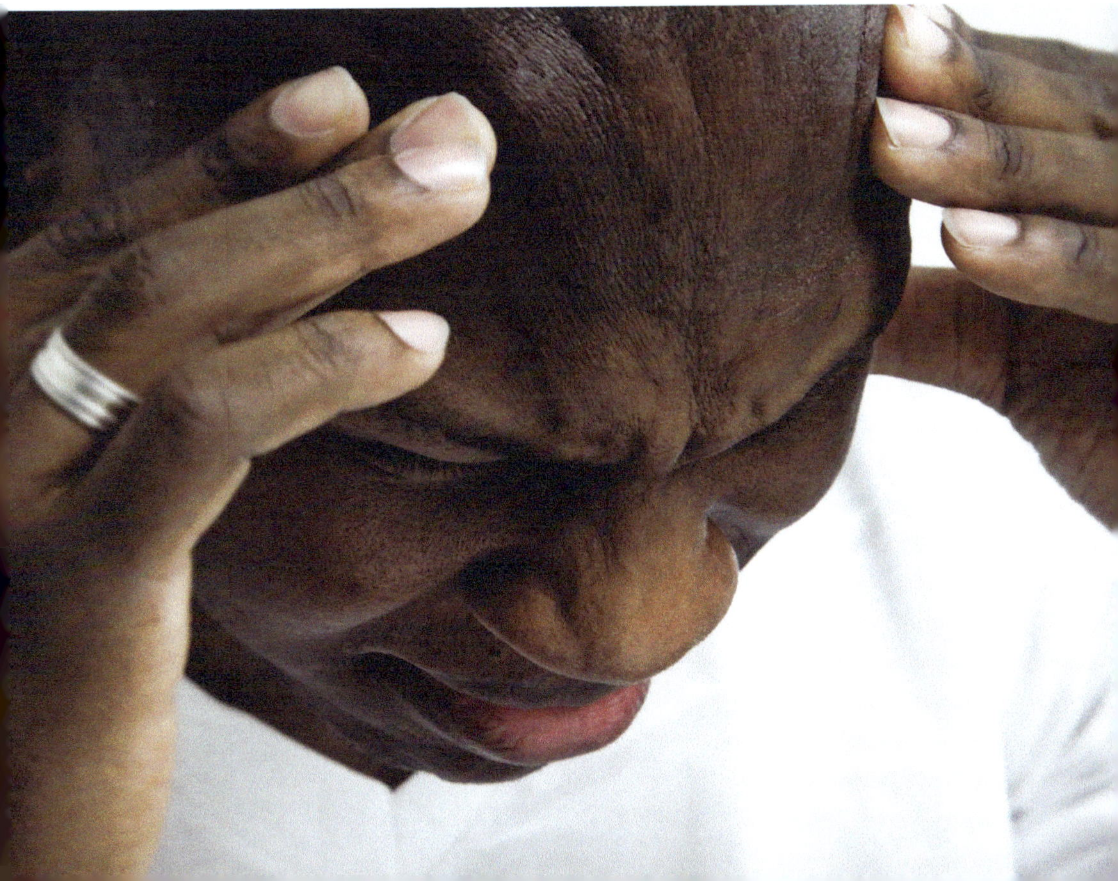

live out their entire lives missing part or all of their memory. The reality of life with amnesia often means placing hope in science and depending on the patience and understanding of loved ones, even if these are people the person with amnesia no longer remembers.

CHAPTER ONE

How the Brain Makes Memories

The human brain may be the most complicated thing in the known world. It is the organ that controls every other part of the body. It makes the heart beat, reminds us to breathe even when we are asleep, and controls the systems that help us to grow from infants to adults. The brain pulls information from everything around us, letting us see, hear, taste, smell, and touch. Perhaps most importantly, the brain allows us to remember.

Memory: The Human Talent

A powerful memory is what sets humans apart from the other animals that share our world. Most creatures have brains that do all the same basic things a human brain can do—feel pain and heat and cold, see and hear things, and sense danger. But only the smartest animals on our planet form memories of these experiences. Only the smartest can learn.

A housefly might land on a hot fireplace, and its brain will tell it to move. But a housefly is not very smart. It might buzz away when it feels the heat, but a moment later, it is likely to come back and land on the same hot fireplace again. A mouse, on the other hand, a more intelligent creature, may run across the fireplace, and his brain, too, will tell him to move. But when the mouse comes through the room again, he will remember that the fireplace was hot. He will take a different path to avoid the fireplace altogether.

Despite its small size, a mouse's brain is able to store information and thus create memories that help the creature navigate its environment.

The mouse's brain created a memory. It gathered many details from the environment around the mouse—not just that the fireplace was hot, but what the fireplace looked like, where it was in the room, and even where the mouse was headed when he scampered across the fireplace to begin with. The mouse's brain stored these details, something the fly's brain could not do. Because of memory, the mouse can learn to run around the fireplace, not across it.

The mouse's ability to learn is remarkable. It proves that even a small brain, in an animal that has relatively little intelligence, can store information. The human brain, by comparison, is capable of everything the mouse brain can do, and endlessly more. Humans do not need to touch a fireplace to know they should avoid it. They have already learned that if something is glowing red, it will probably be hot, and touching it would not be wise. Unlike mice, humans are also curious. Mice do not care about *why* the fire is hot, but the human brain cares. So humans study fire. They remember what they learn. They share their knowledge. They teach their children.

"The brain is a complex biological organ of great computational ability," says Eric R. Kandel, author of *In Search of Memory: The Emergence of a New Science of Mind*. "The brain is responsible not only for relatively simple motor behaviors, such as running and eating, but also for the complex acts that we consider quintessentially human, such as thinking, speaking, and creating works of art."[1]

For most animals, picking up information from the five senses—touch, smell, sight, sound, and taste—is the brain's main job, but in people, the five senses are the tip of the iceberg compared to what the human brain can do.

The Brain's Filing System

Scientists think memory works like a filing cabinet. Every time a sensory experience—a sight, smell, taste, sound, or feeling—passes into the brain through the brain stem, the experience is processed by the brain. If it is important, the brain shuffles the detail to a certain part of the brain, where it is classified with other, similar experiences the brain has processed before.

Finding a memory means the brain must look for it in the right place, with bits of information that are similar. When you struggle to remember a fact or detail, you try to think of things that are linked to it. If you are trying to recall a person's name, you may try to remember where you met. Eventually, you may hit on a detail that was stored in the same "drawer" of your brain's filing cabinet as the person's name, and the forgotten detail will come to you.

"Receiving incoming sensory signals is just the beginning of the brain's work," says Lisa Schoenbrodt in her book *Children with Traumatic Brain Injury: A Parent's Guide*. "What the brain does with the information it receives is what determines the quality of thought and behavior."[2]

Just *how* the brain remembers is something that continues to baffle scientists. It all has to do with the structure of the brain, right down to the tiny cells that create it.

Memory Studies from the Past

Since the late 1700s, scientists have known that electricity powers the brain. Early researchers showed that electrical pulses to a frog's brain could move its legs. As for how electricity forms memories and leads to learning, however, scientists still have much to figure out.

For thousands of years, leading thinkers such as Aristotle believed that the heart, not the brain, was responsible for feelings, learning, and intelligence. Galileo, in the 1600s, thought that human personality and emotions were spiritual and had nothing to do with science. Even the philosopher René Descartes, famous for his saying *I think, therefore I am*, had trouble imagining thoughts and memories as part of the science of the brain. He did not think of the brain as doing both things—reacting to the physical world outside the body *and* creating feelings and new ideas from within.

In the centuries that have passed since these philosophers wrote about human thought and memory, science has discovered that the brain does do both. New technology creates pictures and electrical maps of living, working brains, proving that different parts of the brain work together to do very complicated things. But this organ's amazing abilities still are not completely understood. People with brain disorders such as amnesia are depending on science to get an even better picture of what is happening inside the skull.

"Understanding the human mind in biological terms has emerged as the central challenge for science in the twenty-

Seventeenth-century philosopher René Descartes was among many leading thinkers throughout history who did not connect the function of the brain with human thought and emotion.

first century,"[3] says Kandel. The search for this understanding begins at the bottom of the issue—at the base of the brain.

The Stem of the Matter

The place where the neck meets the head is also where the spinal cord dead-ends into the human brain. This is called the brain stem. In very simple creatures, such as the fly, the brain stem is nearly all there is to the brain. Smarter creatures, such as reptiles, birds, and mammals, have much larger brains with many more parts.

An illustration of the human brain stem shows its placement at the top of the spine. The hindbrain, which is the lowest part of the brain, surrounds the brain stem and is the center of control for basic life functions such as breathing, heart beat, digestion, and movement.

The human brain is more complicated than the brain of any other animal that has ever lived on Earth. Humans have enormous brains. An adult's brain weighs about 3 pounds (1.4kg)—as much as a dozen uncooked hamburger patties. This is much, much larger than the nut-sized brains that sat in the massive skulls of dinosaurs. Human beings are, therefore, much smarter, with brains and thought processes that are much harder to understand. Human thought, says Kandel, is "a set of operations carried out by the brain, much as walking is a set of operations carried out by the legs, except dramatically more complex."[4]

Every human brain has three main parts. The lower section, called the hindbrain, surrounds the brain stem. This area of the brain mostly handles the things people do not have to think about. It reminds the body to breathe in and out every day (and night). It makes the heart beat. After a meal, this part of the brain makes sure the stomach digests the food. It controls reflexes and muscle movements, too. If the hindbrain is injured, the result may be paralysis of the muscles or even death. After all, if the body's control center can no longer tell it to breathe or pump blood, the body will die.

"You can think of the hindbrain as a kind of base camp," says author James S. Nairne. "Not surprisingly, damage to these lower regions of the brain seriously affects the ability of the organism to survive."[5]

The hindbrain also works like a doorway between the body and the rest of the brain. All messages from the body to the brain and from the brain to the body go through the brain stem. The hindbrain is, in some ways, the most important part of the brain. Without it, the body and the rest of the brain will not work as they should. But the hindbrain is also the primitive part of the brain, handling only the simplest jobs, the things that do not require thinking, concentration, and creativity.

More complicated tasks, such as remembering, are done in the midbrain and the forebrain. These activities take a lot of brain power, and they happen somewhere deep in the cerebrum, the biggest part of the brain.

Where Memories Are Made

The cerebrum, the largest part of the brain, has two halves, called hemispheres. Each hemisphere, the right and the left, has four smaller sections called lobes. The lobes help gather information and signals from the body and its environment.

The occipital lobes help make sense of what the eyes see. The parietal lobes take in touching and feeling messages from the skin and joints, giving the body information about where it is, what it is touching, and how it is moving. The temporal lobes receive messages from the ears, important for understanding sounds and for remembering them. Each hemisphere of the cerebrum also has a frontal lobe that makes choices about what the body will do. Unlike the brain stem and hindbrain, which control actions that are not by choice, the frontal lobes are in charge of what a person chooses to do. Eating a third candy bar or pulling someone's hair are actions that come out of the frontal lobe.

The midbrain and the forebrain have other, very vital jobs. One of these is the all-important ability to remember. Scientists think that one brain structure in particular, called the hippocampus, is especially important for human memory.

Each hemisphere of the brain is made up of four lobes: frontal (red), parietal (yellow), occipital (teal), and temporal (green). Additionally, the cerebellum is shown in blue; the brain stem, purple.

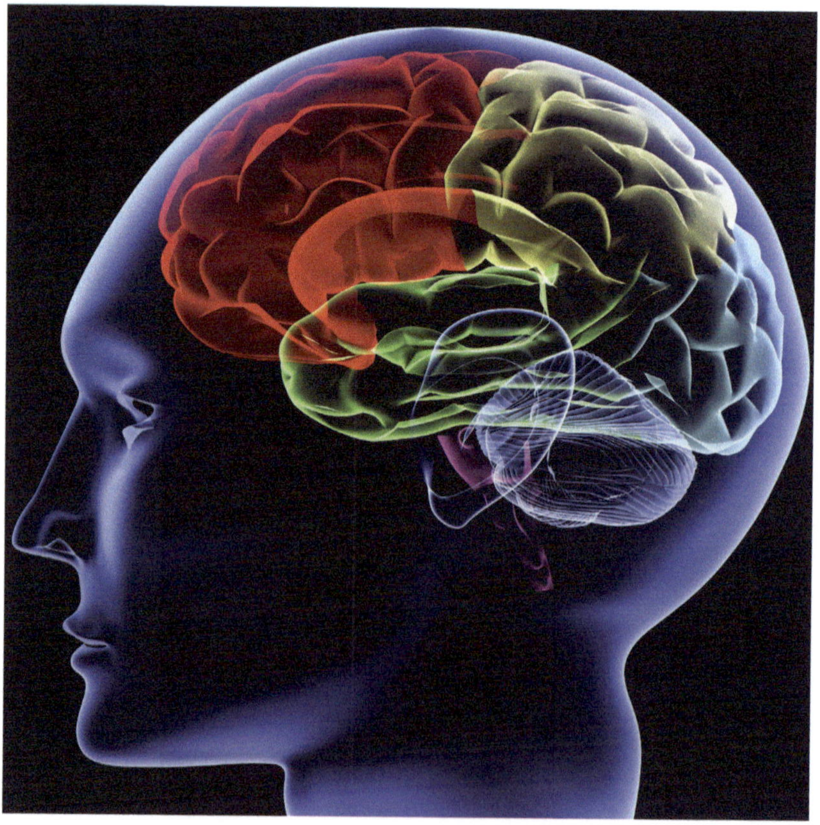

"A number of psychologists and neurobiologists have argued that the hippocampus is a key structure—perhaps *the* key structure—underlying explicit memory for recent experiences in monkeys, humans, and other animals,"[6] says Harvard University psychology professor Daniel L. Schacter in his book, *Searching for Memory: The Brain, the Mind, and the Past.*

Unlike damage to the brain stem, which can cause death, damage to a part of the brain such as a temporal lobe or the hippocampus is usually not deadly—but it can have serious effects on how the brain works. Personality and the way someone thinks, speaks, and understands can be changed forever if any of these parts of the brain are damaged. The way the person remembers, too, can be affected. Damage to the brain can cause changes to the way someone learns and stores information. It can also wipe out memories altogether if the brain cannot conduct the all-important thing that makes memory—electricity.

The Power of the Mind

Like any organ of the body, the brain is made of cells, tiny building blocks so small that they cannot be seen with the naked eye. In the brain, these cells are designed for a single job: to carry electricity. They work like millions of tiny wires to carry messages back and forth to other parts of the brain and to the rest of the body. These are the nerve cells, also called neurons, and they are specially shaped for the task of passing electrical messages. At its center, every neuron has a round cell body that produces the neuron's energy, helps it reproduce, and keeps it alive, but branching out from the cell body are the crucial parts of the neuron: its dendrites and axons.

Dendrites and axons look like plant roots. Under a microscope, in fact, neurons look very much like trees that have lost their leaves during winter. A dendrite is a branch that brings electrical signals into the neuron, and an axon is a branch that sends electrical signals out to other nerve cells. Neurons are like trees in a forest, says Diane Ackerman in her book, *An Alchemy of Mind: The Marvel and Mystery of the Brain*—and they talk among themselves.

"For that purpose," Ackerman says, "they have two kinds of limbs, dendrites and axons: the former to listen, the latter to speak." Dendrites, she says, "hear what neighboring neurons signal through their axons."[7]

Each neuron is arranged so that its "branches"—its dendrites and axons—touch the branches of other neurons. The place where branches touch is called a synapse. Electricity passes through synapses, jumping from the axon of one neuron to the dendrite of another, at 200 miles per hour (322kmph). Because there are trails of neurons throughout the body, connecting the brain to fingers and toes, eyes and ears, nose and tongue, the brain can quickly send messages anywhere in the body.

Telegrams to the Brain

Every part of the body can also send speedy messages back to the brain. These messages do not go just anywhere. They are instantly shuffled to the part of the brain that will know what to do with them.

"This system allows us to link the varied components of everyday episodes into integrated records of experiences: what we hear, what we think, and how we feel,"[8] says Schacter.

Many scientists think of the brain like a computer, gathering input, coding it for storage, and filing it away in the proper place. Like a computer, the brain has different kinds of "software," and these all have different jobs. Some of these jobs are to take in signals, such as a hot fireplace, and help the body to respond by moving away. Other jobs, however, seem to involve making, not just receiving, electrical signals. This is what sets a brain apart from a computer and baffles scientists who study the nervous system. The brain invents new thoughts and can imagine false ones. It lets humans feel physical pain, but also emotions such as love and hate.

The Memory Mystery

Scientists are still learning how the brain does its most complicated work—forming memories—and where in the brain this process happens. All human beings are born with a complete set of neurons. Scientists believe that as experiences and senses send electrical pulses through the cells of the brain, these cells move around to make it easier for the same kinds of pulses to come through the next time. The brain gets faster at moving along that particular message.

Neurons actually rearrange themselves with each new sensory experience. They line up differently every time a new electrical charge passes along their branches. This way, the experience that caused the charge will be more familiar to the neurons when it happens again. It is as though the neurons say to one another, "We have seen a pulse like this before. Step aside to let it through." When this happens, a "memory" of that particular experience is formed.

An illustration depicts the exchange of electrical impulses among nerve cells in the brain, which can result in the creation of memory.

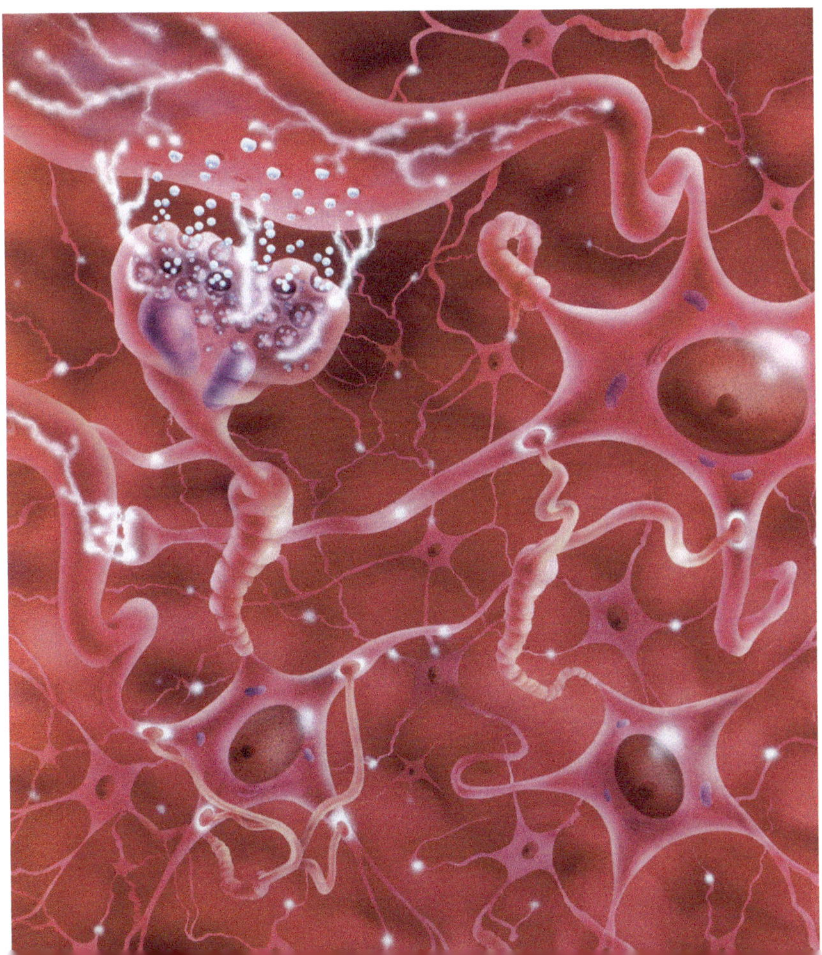

"The brain's billions of cells are engaged in a continuous, frenetic dance of activity," says Nairne. "From what seem to be chaotic patterns of cellular activity arise the intricacies of human behavior, thought, emotion, and creativity."[9]

It is impossible to overestimate the value of this ability to remember. Memory lets people recognize their loved ones. Memory tells people what is dangerous and what is safe. Memory lets people sing along with their favorite songs. Memory even makes it possible to read words like the ones on this page. A reader without a memory would have forgotten the beginning of this sentence by now.

The neurons in the brain are constantly changing positions every time a person smells, hears, tastes, sees, and touches. Neurons are constantly replacing the old experiences with the new. No two people ever have the same experiences, in the same order, from birth. Therefore, no two brains are the same. In a healthy brain, new memories are being made every moment, and many of these memories are stored by the brain for life. It is a remarkable ability. Very old people still recall things from early childhood, even after their brains have spent decades recording new details, nonstop, every single day.

The brain's method of remembering is incredibly complicated. Like a computer with its many file folders and destinations for information, there seems to be no single area of the brain that is responsible for storing all memories.

"Memory is a *process* rather than a *place* in the brain," says Schoenbrodt. "There is not a single, unitary memory 'storage vault,' located in a specific area of the brain."[10]

Just the same, scientists have learned that certain parts of the brain, such as the temporal lobes and the hippocampus, seem to be especially important areas for making and storing memories. This knowledge comes from studying people whose memory has somehow gone terribly wrong.

The Case of HM

In the 1950s, one patient, now famous to anyone who has studied memory and the brain, showed scientists just how important

Flashbulb Memory, or Déjà Vu?

A memory "illusion" is when the brain is tricked into thinking it has seen or done something before. The result is the strange feeling of déjà vu—a sudden sense that something is very familiar, even though you cannot remember having experienced it before. Scientists think the phenomenon happens when you have had a prior experience that is very similar, but your brain never made a concrete memory of it. You are left with a "shadow" of a memory, and the false sense that you have been in the exact same situation before.

The opposite situation may be what brain experts call "flashbulb" memories—sharper than average memories of emotional times in life. For example, many people claim they can remember exactly where they were, what they were doing, what they were wearing, or even what they were eating when they heard that terrorists had flown planes into the World Trade Center on 9/11. These sharp, emotionally charged memories are called flashbulb memories, and they usually do not fade away with time.

certain parts of the brain are to making and keeping memories. The patient became known by his initials, HM, and his amnesia was so extreme that he has since lived his life without being able to make any new memories at all.

HM had epilepsy, a condition that causes seizures—episodes of jerking, shaking, and loss of consciousness that come on suddenly and without warning. HM's seizures were so bad that in 1953, when he was twenty-seven years old, he had surgery. Doctors took out the parts of HM's brain that they believed were causing his seizures. Parts of HM's hippocampus and temporal lobes were removed. While he recovered, it seemed the surgery was a success. HM's seizures were not as bad. He was just as smart he had been before the operation. The surgery did not seem to have caused any problems, except one: HM could not remember anything after his operation.

"If his doctors went out of his sight for even a few minutes and then returned, H. M. couldn't recall having ever seen them before and had to be reintroduced," says Richard M. Restak, author of *The Modular Brain*. "He could still recall those things he learned before the operation, but he could not retain any new information for more than a few seconds."[11]

For HM, life after the surgery has been very different than it was before the surgery. As soon as his lunch plate is cleared from the table, he forgets not only what he ate, but also that he has eaten lunch at all. He promptly forgets every person he meets. He greets the doctors and nurses he sees several times a day as if he were meeting them for the first time.

Now in his eighties, HM can remember what year he was born, but for most of his life, he has had no idea of his age. When someone tells him his mother has passed away, he cries and grieves as if it is the first time he has heard the news—even if he was told the same thing the day before.

There has never been any doubt that HM is still intelligent. After his surgery, he could still carry on a perfectly normal conversation with anyone. He just could not remember it five minutes later.

Because of an operation to solve one problem, HM has lived for decades with a different problem. He will never again form a new memory that lasts longer than a few moments. Missing the parts of his brain that are necessary for normal memory, he has lived a life that probably makes very little sense to him, and he must often feel very confused and lonely.

Brain Experiments: Few and Far Between

Despite having no memory himself, HM will always be remembered. As sad as his story is, HM is famous to scientists because, for the first time, doctors had a chance to see what happened to a living person when specific parts of his brain were removed. This is not the kind of experiment researchers normally perform on living people. Taking out chunks of someone's brain just to see what would happen is not ethical. But HM taught scientists a great deal about how the brain makes and stores memory, in what parts of the brain this happens, and how injury to the brain can affect a person's ability to remember things and make new memories. HM gave scientists their first good look at the phenomenon of memory loss, known as amnesia.

CHAPTER TWO

What Is Amnesia?

On January 12, 2005, a young man in his late teens was found in a dirty snowbank in the town of Weymouth, Massachusetts. He had suffered a head injury. He was treated at a hospital and was then sent to a homeless shelter. The man had no memory of his name, where he was from, how he had ended up in the snowbank, or anything else that had happened to him before he was discovered lying dazed in the snow. He was taken in by a woman who gave him a place to stay until he could remember who he was or until his family could find him—if he had a family at all.

"I just want to have my memory back," he said. "I hope someone is looking for me."[12]

This is one of very few true stories of amnesia that reads like a book or a movie script, but it is easy to see why there *are* so many movies about amnesia. What could be more interesting than a person who wanders into town with no idea who he is or how he got there? The reality is that people with amnesia are just regular people with an unusual problem. They have lost a chunk of memory, and with it, part or all of their identity.

The human brain is very complicated. The process of how it makes and stores memories is not well understood, and therefore, the way memories are lost is also not well understood. People suffering from amnesia are victims of a very perplexing problem that may have no solution.

Memory Loss Comes in Many Forms

Amnesia is a very general word describing any loss of memory. There are, however, different types of memory, so there are also different types of amnesia. The amnesia that affected HM so that he could not learn or remember anything new was very different from the amnesia that affected the young man in the snowbank, who could learn and remember everything *after* his accident but nothing before. Understanding which part of the brain has been damaged, whether by accident or illness, sometimes helps doctors figure out what type of memory a patient with amnesia has lost. Sometimes, patients and their doctors must simply wait to see which memories return and which do not.

One of the most puzzling things about any kind of amnesia is that it usually only affects certain kinds of memory. Some patients lose long-term memories. Some lose the ability to form

While amnesia can affect a person's ability to recall past memories or create new ones, it rarely results in the loss of basic skills and habits.

short-term memories and learn new things. Some people lose explicit knowledge—the facts and the memories of specific experiences that make up their personal history. But for some reason, implicit memories, the skills and habits a person does without thinking, are rarely lost.

Scientists use these facts as proof that the memory process involves most or all of the brain. Damage to one part of the brain may wipe out one type of memory but not others. Amnesia leaves most people nearly whole and mostly normal—except for a chunk of missing memories.

The Long and Short of Memory

Just as the brain is a master at remembering, it is also very good at forgetting, even when a person does not have amnesia. A huge amount of information goes into the brain every day. Most of this—the color of a pebble in the driveway, the number of swallows it took to finish a glass of orange juice in the morning—is information a person will never need. The brain is very good at sorting out the important things and dumping all the rest to make room for memories that will be made tomorrow.

"Much learning in daily life can be labeled 'updating,'" says Robert W. Howard in his book, *Learning and Memory: Major Ideas, Principles, Issues and Applications*. With time, he explains, a person's knowledge about various things must change to stay current. "Destructive updating," he says, "is getting rid of no longer current information."[13]

When the brain decides a detail is worth keeping, at least for a while, it sorts the information into a memory for the short-term or for the long-term. Short-term memories are things the brain will probably use again soon. These are the details that help someone plan a day or a week, for example. If a teacher says there will be a spelling test tomorrow, students will need to store that information, at least until tomorrow. They probably will not need to remember the conversation in ten years, so this may become a short-term memory, one that is forgotten when it is no longer needed. Short-term memory is hard at work during a movie, too, forming memories of what happened

Short-term memory is what allows movie goers to follow the course of a film's plot, allowing the recall of what happens at the beginning so that the end makes sense.

at the beginning so that everything makes sense at the end. The brain quickly forgets the name of the movie's producer, which appeared in the credits at the start of the film, but when the movie is over, the brain forms a long-term memory of watching it. This memory will probably exist for life.

"It seems unlikely that long-term memories fade as a simple by-product of time," says author James S. Nairne. "New memories compete and interfere with recovery of the old," he explains, but with the right kind of cues, "previously forgotten material becomes refreshed and available for use once again."[14]

Over time, as a person gets older and learns new things, the brain stores a lot of information in its long-term memory. Some of the memories are facts and some are skills. Together, these

Erase This, Please

It is hard to imagine anyone wanting to lose his or her memory. People who have lived through something very terrible, however, sometimes wish they could wipe out their memories of that one event. In April 2007 French and American scientists reported finding a medication that might be able to do just that. Rats that were trained to be afraid of a certain sound were given the drug, and afterward, the same sound no longer frightened them. The scientists believe that when a bad memory is pulled out of long-term storage in the brain, the drug might be able to prevent it from being stored again. Thus, the bad memory could be forgotten, while no other memories would be destroyed. If this medication were to work the same way in humans, there might one day be a cure for the terrible mental effects of war, natural disasters, accidents, and other terrifying events.

make up the two types of long-term memory, one of which happens to be much more vulnerable to amnesia than the other.

Implicit and Explicit Memory

The brain is able to form two main kinds of long-term knowledge. One of the brain's main tasks is remembering how to *do* things. The brain's other job is keeping track of what is *known*. Scientists often describe these two types of memory as the difference between "knowing how" and "knowing that."

Knowing *how* is called implicit memory, or procedural memory. It is the memory of a procedure, or how to do a certain thing. Riding a bicycle is one example. It can take a lot of practice and a lot of skinned knees to learn how to ride a bike, but once the brain has learned, it does not forget. The phrase *it's just like riding a bike* is based on science—once the brain knows how to do something, it stores this knowledge for life. A person who has not climbed onto a bike for years will be able to place his feet on the pedals, and without thinking about it, ride around the block. The brain has stored this memory, and it is implicit: A person does not have to think about how to ride a bike.

People have many implicit memories, usually for the things they spend a lot of time practicing. Riding a skateboard, reading a book, or playing the piano are examples of implicit memories. Once a person masters these skills, she can do them without thinking about them. She does not need to learn them again every time.

"Information in implicit memory is unconsciously held, resists forgetting, shows little transfer beyond training stimuli, and is acquired through practice,"[15] says Howard.

The other type of long-term memory is called explicit memory, or declarative memory. Explicit memories are things we can declare or talk about. These are the facts we learn over time. If implicit memory is knowing *how*, explicit memory is knowing *what*. This is the kind of memory created when

Implicit memory, or procedural memory, is what allows a person to retain a skill once it's learned, so that a person who learns to ride a bike as a child is still able to do so as an adult.

someone studies for a test. Instead of practicing a skill, he is memorizing facts.

Explicit memories are usually things people have to think about. Recalling presents from a birthday years ago might take a while. The brain stores many facts for the long-term, but that gets to be an awful lot of information over time. Brains have to work harder to find information from long ago.

"Information in the explicit system is consciously available," says Howard, but "is prone to forgetting."[16]

The brain seems to store different types of knowledge and facts in different places and in different ways. Amnesia usually causes the loss only of certain memories or certain types of memory. This leads to different types of amnesia. The two forms of amnesia that are perhaps most troubling for their victims, and the most difficult for doctors to understand, usually come from some kind of head injury, and they involve the loss of memories made either before or after that event.

Anteretrograde Amnesia: The Loss of Memory-Making Abilities

At age twenty-seven, the young man known as HM lost his ability to remember anything new. From the day of his brain surgery forward, he could not form new memories. He has continued living for many years after the surgery, but as far as his brain is concerned, his memorable life lasted twenty-seven years, and not a day more.

The loss of the ability to remember any new facts or events after amnesia sets in is called anteretrograde amnesia. It is usually caused by damage to the brain, whether from an injury or a medical condition. A person with anteretrograde amnesia, such as HM, cannot remember any new information. Memories of recent experiences quickly disappear, although the person can clearly remember things that happened before the brain injury.

"The key to understanding patients like H. M. is realizing that their disorders are highly selective," says Harvard University psychology professor Daniel L. Schacter. "Various kinds of knowledge and skills are all spared."[17]

For patients like HM, who have anteretrograde amnesia, the condition may be more difficult for their loved ones than for them. After all, these patients may forget that they cannot remember.

"There is a kind of poetic justice at work for patients with [anteretrograde] amnesia," says Schacter. "The impairment might mercifully serve a protective function by preventing patients from becoming aware of the catastrophic nature of their memory loss."[18] Sadly, this is not the case for all people with amnesia.

Retrograde Amnesia: The Loss of Memories Themselves

The man who was found in a Massachusetts snowbank could be described as the opposite of HM, in terms of memory loss. This man, who could recall nothing before waking up in a snowbank, is a victim of retrograde amnesia. This form of amnesia wipes out long-term memories stored in the brain, or at least, it blocks the brain's ability to find them.

Unlike HM, the man in the snowbank was perfectly able to learn new things and form new memories. He made a friend at the homeless shelter and remembered not only her name but her phone number. He was able to recall everything that happened to him after he was found in the snow. But he knew absolutely nothing of his past. He did not remember his name or his birthday, his family members or his hometown. He did not know if he had brothers or sisters or if his parents were still alive. He could not name a single hobby he had before or a sport he could play (although quite possibly, if he had been a guitar player before, he might well have remembered the implicit skills of what to do with the instrument if one was placed in his hands).

One of the most interesting things about retrograde amnesia is that only certain kinds of long-term memories disappear. The person with this kind of amnesia has not lost *everything* he or

Retrograde amnesia affects the ability to recall memories from the past.

she ever learned before. The man in the snowbank could still talk, for example. The years of new words he had been learning since birth were still in his memory. He did not wake up in the snow with the mental abilities of an infant. Indeed, he walked, talked, and acted every bit like the grown man he was. He simply had no memory of the process of growing up, or of the accident that robbed him of his memories.

Living with retrograde amnesia must be very difficult. Imagine the frustration of waking up each day knowing that your past has vanished, and try as you might, you simply cannot get it back. In her book, *Past Forgetting: My Memory Lost and Found*, amnesia sufferer Jill Robinson describes what it is like to live with amnesia: "I walk through the dark driveway to my house. I open the door. The house is dark and still and empty. I walk through each room and not only is nothing here, I don't even remember what was here."[19] Amnesia made her feel like a stranger in her own life.

Transient Global Amnesia

Because they are usually caused by damage to the brain, retrograde and anteretrograde amnesias are especially frightening—these memory problems can be permanent. Movies and soap operas featuring people with amnesia are often misleading, because characters may get back all of their memories or their ability to make new ones. When the brain has been damaged, this does not always happen.

There are times, however, when the brain does recover from amnesia, and memories can be restored. One type of amnesia, called transient global amnesia, has no known cause at all. It is a sudden, severe, but temporary loss of memory. According to the staff of the Mayo Clinic, during an episode of transient global amnesia, "your recall of events simply vanishes, so you can't remember where you are or how you got there . . . you do remember who you are, and you recognize family members and others you have known for a long time, but that knowledge doesn't make your memory loss any less disturbing."[20]

Transient global amnesia strikes with no warning. Although this kind of amnesia sometimes follows a shocking event such as getting bad news or jumping into a very cold swimming pool, there is no definite cause. Fortunately, these episodes are very rare, and when they do happen, they do not last long. A person who has experienced this type of amnesia once will probably never have it again.

"Episodes of transient global amnesia last only six hours, on average," say experts at the Mayo Clinic. When an episode is over, "you remember nothing that happened while your memory was impaired, and you might not recall the hours beforehand. Otherwise, though, your memory is fine."[21]

Transient global amnesia gives its victims a glimpse into the life of someone who lives with permanent memory problems. Because the condition is temporary, sufferers of transient global amnesia do get their memories back. But every case of amnesia serves as a reminder that memory is a very fragile and mysterious thing. Even when a brain injury has never happened, memories might be lost simply because the brain has

False Confessions

Memories are not always that reliable. (Anyone who has aced a test in school and forgotten all the information by the next day can confirm this.) The idea of amnesia sometimes leads to false confessions—when people admit to crimes they did not commit.

In a police interrogation room, a nervous suspect who had nothing to do with a crime might begin to doubt his own memories. The interrogator asking the questions might suggest that the suspect "forgot" committing the crime, and the suspect might begin to fear that he really did have amnesia for a short while. He might even confess to the crime, although his statements will usually be as foggy as his false memories: "I guess I must have done it, then."

Fortunately, such false confessions do not always hold up when questioned in court.

reached some sort of overload. The brain can force forgetfulness on itself when the pain of a certain experience or memory is simply too overwhelming.

Psychogenic Amnesia

After natural disasters or other ordeals that cause trauma to a great many people, psychiatrists often see a rise in the number of patients seeking treatment for mental or emotional problems. Some of these patients are troubled by memories of the terrible event they have experienced. Other patients may be having the opposite problem—they cannot remember anything about the horrifying experience at all.

The sudden loss of memory that is linked to an extremely disturbing, often life-threatening experience is called psychogenic amnesia. Scientists have been studying cases of this kind of forgetting since the 1870s. By the end of the nineteenth century, "psychiatry had become alerted to the pathogenic influence of persistent memories (both conscious and unconscious) of traumatic events," say Martin T. Orne and his colleagues in their article, "Reconstructing Memory Through Hypnosis."[22]

Psychogenic amnesia tends to happen to people who have no history of mental illness but who have lived through something terrifying, such as an earthquake, getting mugged, or a violent battle during a war. Most people who have psychogenic amnesia realize that they have lost some of their memory. Usually, the missing memories are of the traumatic event itself and/or a short period of time right after it. Brain injury is not the cause of this kind of amnesia. (If a brain injury *did* occur, the amnesia would be classified differently.) Many doctors and scientists who study cases of psychogenic amnesia believe that it is caused by the brain itself as protection against memories so painful or troubling that the person would not be able to cope with them.

"Indeed," says Dr. Theodore G. Brna Jr., "psychogenic amnesia often improves spontaneously with apparent resolution of the underlying conflict."[23]

Like most other forms of memory loss, psychogenic amnesia is not well understood. However, this type of amnesia, in particular, is interesting to many people dealing with difficult situations or emotional troubles they cannot seem to explain. Studies show that half of all murderers claim to have had some kind of psychiatric amnesia when they committed their crime, and there has been a recent increase in the number of troubled adults who seek help to uncover memories of childhood abuse that they suspect have been buried by their own brains.

Healing or Hype?

Although there is truth to some of the claims that buried memories cause people's social problems, skeptical researchers believe that many people seeking lost memories actually find false ones instead. In effect, a psychotherapist can talk someone into creating memories of events that never really happened. For example, says psychology professor and memory expert Elizabeth F. Loftus, "not a single piece of empirical work in human memory supports the authenticity of claims going

Some amnesia patients enter psychotherapy in order to explore repressed memories, but experts are skeptical of the accuracy of such recollections.

back to six months of age." Loftus says research has found "no controlled studies showing an event can be accurately reproduced in memory after a long period of repression."[24]

In other words, an infant who is frightened or troubled by something probably will not grow into a frightened or troubled adult with amnesia just because of that one experience. But believers and skeptics alike have a lot of gray area to sift through in studying memory. Very little is known about the causes and effects of amnesia of any type. All that is known is that memory loss does occur, and when it happens, there may be little that scientists or doctors can do to restore the lost memories.

One of the best ways to deal with amnesia is to keep it from happening in the first place. Much of the current work on amnesia is focused on teaching people about common causes of amnesia and how to keep their brains safe from such hardships.

CHAPTER THREE

What Causes Amnesia?

Amnesia is not a disease. One person cannot pass it to another, and it is not hereditary, handed down through families from one generation to the next. It can be a symptom of an illness, as in the forgetfulness of Alzheimer's disease. It can be the result of a bad accident in which the head gets injured, or it can be caused by drugs, alcohol, or even poor nutrition when a person's diet is missing important nutrients. Amnesia can also be caused by traumatic emotional events, as in the case of psychogenic forgetting.

"Memory problems resulting from brain trauma can vary widely in nature and extent," says author Lisa Schoenbrodt. "The processes involved in memory are very complex. Damage to any part of this intricate system can disrupt your ability to categorize, link, and recall past experiences."[25]

Because amnesia is not a disease, and because there are so many types of amnesia and so many possible causes, it is hard for scientists to find cures or treatments. The best way to deal with memory loss may be to prevent the things that cause it. Therefore, scientists actively study known causes of amnesia in the hope that they can stop brain damage from happening in the first place.

Traumatic Brain Injury

The brain has the best protection the body can provide. It is buried within the thick, bony shield of the skull, where it is surrounded by fluid so that when the head moves, the delicate brain does not constantly bump against the skull. It is a very

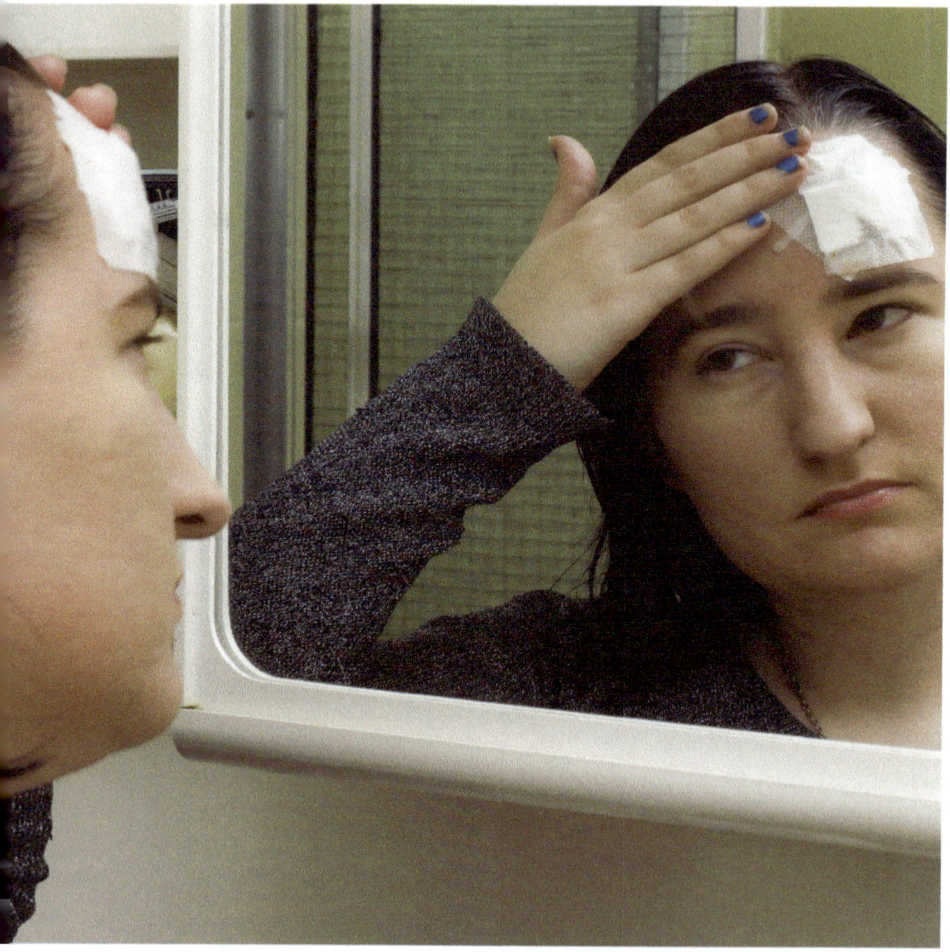

Because of its size and weight, the human head is susceptible to injury. A blow to the head can result in traumatic brain injury, which is one of the most common causes of amnesia.

effective safety system. Despite this, anything that hurts the head can hurt the brain, and the way people are shaped makes the human head more vulnerable to injury than the heads of most animals.

For one thing, humans stand upright. For the size of the feet on which they balance, humans are naturally rather top-heavy. If someone stumbles and falls, the head comes from the greatest height, so it is the body part that hits the ground the hardest.

Human heads also perch on longer, more wobbly necks than the heads of many animals. (Giraffes and storks are two good exceptions, but giraffes walk steadily on four legs, and a stork's brain is not big, so its head simply is not that heavy.) The heavy human head can whip backward or forward on the end of the neck during a fall, causing injury to the spinal cord. Although other primates, such as gorillas and chimpanzees, also have quite large brains, their necks are shorter and thicker than a human's, and they spend more time squatting than standing, so the risk of a head injury from a stumble is minimal. Humans are unique in the animal kingdom in that they have a very high risk of head injury.

"Although growing a big neocortex gave us 'book smarts,'" say Temple Grandin and Catherine Johnson, authors of *Animals in Translation: Using the Mysteries of Autism to Decode Animal Behavior*, "we paid a price. For one thing, bigger frontal lobes probably made humans a lot more vulnerable to brain damage and dysfunction of just about any kind."[26]

Human beings also place themselves in far more dangerous situations than other animals do. A monkey travels only as fast as its body is designed to go. People, on the other hand, have invented machines to help them reach incredible speeds. Bicycles, motorcycles, cars, and planes, for example, allow humans to travel at speeds far greater than their bodies are designed to go. The impact of a crash at such speeds can be serious and sometimes fatal.

During such an accident, the head all too often gets the worst of the damage. The brain rattles around inside the skull, smashing against the bone. When the brain is injured this way, it is called a concussion, which means "violent shaking." The result is traumatic brain injury, one of the most common and most serious causes of amnesia. The two main symptoms of traumatic brain injury are loss of consciousness and a period of memory loss after the injury, called posttraumatic amnesia (PTA).

"A patient with a concussion may display any combination of . . . signs and symptoms," says author and doctor Robert C.

Cantu, in an article in the *Journal of Athletic Training*. "Many consider the duration of PTA the best indicator of traumatic brain injury severity."[27]

PTA can be retrograde or anteretrograde, depending on whether there is a loss of memories from before the accident or a loss of the ability to remember new things afterward. According to Cantu, "we now know that structural damage with loss of brain cells does occur with some concussions." Anteretrograde memory, he says, "is frequently the last function to return after the recovery from a loss of consciousness."[28] In many patients whose head injury was very severe, memory may never be completely normal again.

"The most common cognitive impairment among severely head-injured patients is memory loss,"[29] says Sandra J. Judd in *Brain Disorders Sourcebook*. About 270,000 people in the United States each year have a traumatic brain injury, she says, and 80,000 of them "live with significant disability as a result of the injury."[30]

Because most traumatic brain injuries are caused by accidents, they are very random and difficult to prevent. Safety is the best way to avoid brain injuries that can cause lifelong amnesia. Simply wearing a seatbelt in the car and putting on a helmet when using bikes, skateboards, and other equipment would prevent thousands of serious brain injuries. Unfortunately, not all cases of amnesia are this preventable.

Head Injuries: The Statistics

Every year, three quarters of a million people in the United States spend time in a hospital because of a head injury. Seventy percent of them have posttraumatic amnesia, and 30 percent of these lose some or all of their memory for at least four weeks. The longer amnesia lasts after a head injury, the smaller the chances that the person will recover all of his or her memory.

Amnesia from Disease

Brain damage does not always come from reckless behavior or unfortunate accidents. Sometimes, illness is to blame. Perhaps the best-known and most wicked thief of memory is Alzheimer's disease. More than 4 million Americans are losing their memories to this illness. Although there are a few cases of Alzheimer's disease in people younger than sixty years of age, it usually strikes in one's sixties, seventies, or eighties. It is a disease of the brain's cells. Proteins begin to clump together in the neurons, and as a result, the cells die. Dead and dying brain cells stick together in clumps, called plaques, and these block important electrical messages from getting around the brain.

A scan of a healthy brain, left, is compared to that of an Alzheimer's patient, which is significantly shrunken and degenerated. As the brain cells die, the patient suffers an increasing loss of memory and function.

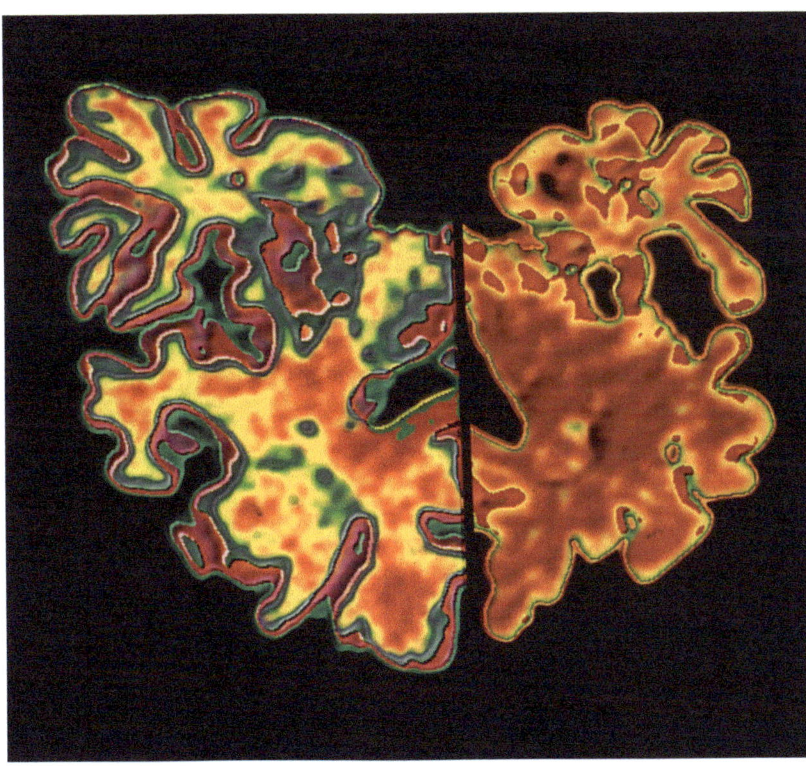

When the brain's cells cannot communicate with each other, the brain loses the ability to do important jobs. Memory is one of the first things to go. People with Alzheimer's often start to lose their memories even before they know they have the disease. When this memory loss begins to be a problem for daily living, it is called dementia.

"People with dementia may have difficulty learning new things or remembering the names of people they just met," says Dr. Alberto Maud. "They may get lost in places that were previously very familiar or have trouble finding words."[31]

The amnesia caused by Alzheimer's is both retrograde and anteretrograde. Patients forget what they knew, and they also lose the ability to learn anything new. They start to ask the same questions over and over because they forget the answers as soon as they hear them. They slowly start to lose memories of their past, too. A person with Alzheimer's disease may eventually forget her entire life since childhood, and may therefore begin to believe that she is still a child. Memory loss is such a major part of Alzheimer's disease that some people think amnesia itself is the disease. It is not—it is only a symptom. But it is usually the first sign that a person has Alzheimer's, and it certainly is the biggest problem of the disease.

"It is frightening to lose control of your body in any way," says Alzheimer's sufferer Thomas DeBaggio in his book, *Losing My Mind: An Intimate Look at Life with Alzheimer's*. "It is especially tragic when the body's central control system, the brain, is the target of an angry destructive process that science has been unable to tame or reclaim. Memories tell us who we are and where we have been. . . . My memories are slowly disappearing."[32]

Doctors have not found a cure for Alzheimer's. They do not yet know how to prevent it. There are medications that can slow it down, but love and patience are still the best tools people have to help someone who suffers from this kind of progressive and merciless memory loss.

A Sudden Strike on Memory

Amnesia can come on slowly, as it does in Alzheimer's disease and other illnesses like it. Accidents, on the other hand, happen suddenly, and so does the memory loss they can cause. Traumatic brain injuries and concussions are the result of accidents that happen outside the body, but other types of brain "accidents" happen within the brain itself. These are called cerebro-

A color-enhanced CAT scan of a human brain shows an area of dead tissue (red) resulting from a stroke, a leading cause of brain damage that can affect motor function and memory and can even cause death.

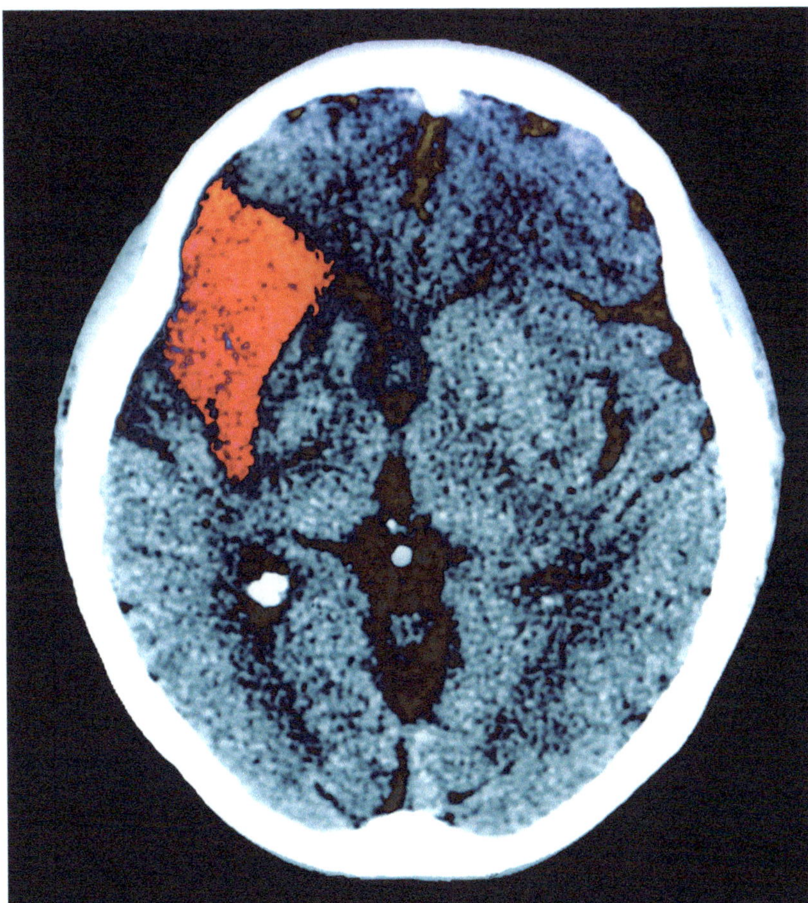

vascular accidents, or CVAs—literally, accidents within the blood vessels of the brain. A simpler word for a CVA is a stroke.

Like every part of the body, the brain depends on blood for oxygen and nutrients. A stroke happens when the blood supply to part of the brain is cut off. A blood vessel might form a clog, called a clot. Blood cannot get past the clot, and when part of the brain goes without oxygen for a while, that part no longer works properly. Without blood and nutrients, cells of the brain die, and often, they take memory with them.

Strokes are a leading cause of brain damage. Many problems are created in the body if the brain cannot send messages to the right places. Some people who have had a major stroke cannot move one of their hands or cannot smile with one side of their mouth. Strokes can also cause loss of memory for past events, as well as the loss of implicit memory for how to do things. People who have had a stroke often struggle to remember the right words for everyday objects such as a pencil or a chair. They may forget how to read or write.

"It is estimated that approximately one third of stroke victims will develop memory problems," says Maud. "The memory problems can be so severe that they interfere with normal functioning and are then called dementia."[33]

Most strokes are caused by blocked blood vessels. A healthy heart and a healthy cardiovascular system, therefore, are important for prevention throughout life. Lawrence H. Wyatt, writing in the *Journal of the American Chiropractic Association*, says strokes can happen at any age. "In the United States, strokes are the most common cause of disability and the third most common cause of death in adults," he says. "Especially prone to stroke are people with unhealthy lifestyles—those who smoke, stick to poor diets, and don't exercise."[34]

The causes of strokes are known, and there are things people can do to prevent them. Education, therefore, might help prevent many cases of stroke-related amnesia. The same is true for another cause of major memory loss: alcoholism.

Memories Lost to Alcohol Abuse

Drinking alcohol affects the brain and the nervous system. A person who has had too much to drink will start to show it. Slurred speech, stumbling, slow reflexes, and poor reasoning skills are signs that alcohol has had some bad effects on the brain. Alcoholic beverages can also cause amnesia. People who have had way too much to drink might even black out, waking up the next day with no idea where they are or how they got there. Such a situation may be scary at the time. With any luck, it will convince the person not to drink so much in the future. Although the memories of that particular night are probably lost forever, the person will move on with no lasting effects on future memory.

Alcohol's effects on the brain are not always temporary. Alcoholics, people who are addicted to alcohol, can sometimes get permanent amnesia—not just for the events of one evening but for life. The condition is called Wernicke-Korsakoff syndrome or Korsakoff's psychosis. Over time, heavy use of alcohol can affect the body's ability to use thiamine, also known as vita-

Drinking too much alcohol can have both temporary and long-term effects on memory.

Where Am I?

In September 2006 Jeff Ingram left his home in Olympia, Washington, to visit family and friends in Canada. He never arrived. Instead, he wound up on the streets of Denver, Colorado, with no idea where he was—or who he was. When he finally found a hospital, he had trouble getting admitted because he could not give them his name.

Ingram was suffering a type of amnesia called dissociative fugue, a total memory blank that usually goes along with wandering far from home. More than a month went by before Ingram finally made his way to a Denver TV station and appeared on the network news to plead for someone to recognize him. Halfway across the country, his fiancée was watching. Ingram went home, but he had no memories of the place. He and his fiancée married, but he had no memories of the years they dated. The cause of his fugue was not known.

The car Ingram was driving when he left Olympia was never found.

Jeff Ingram of Olympia, Washington, was suffering from amnesia and did not remember his name, home town, or any other details from his past when he turned up in Denver, Colorado, in September 2006. The next month, he appeared at a television news conference in the hope that a viewer would recognize him.

min B1. When the brain does not have enough of this important vitamin, the memory process is damaged. Patients who have a long-term history of alcohol abuse, Harvard University psychology professor Daniel L. Schacter says, "show a profound loss of memory for recent experiences." He adds that "in addition to memory loss, most patients with Korsakoff's syndrome have cognitive and emotional problems."[35]

Korsakoff's psychosis is a permanent form of amnesia. A person who has this condition often tries to hide memory loss by making up stories for experiences or situations he or she cannot remember. But even for the best storytellers, the damage to the brain has been done, and the memories are lost forever.

Korsakoff's psychosis gets worse over time, even if the person completely stops drinking. When the body's ability to use thiamine is lost because of alcohol abuse, this ability cannot be recovered. A memory-erasing chain of events has been set in motion, and there is no way to stop it. Even taking vitamin supplements will not help. Wernicke-Korsakoff syndrome continues to get worse and memories continue to fade until eventually, the syndrome causes death. As with so many other causes of amnesia, there is no cure.

Contagious Culprits

Amnesia is usually brought on by diseases, injuries, or conditions that are not contagious. Alzheimer's disease does not pass from one person to the next through a cough or a sneeze, and a person will not have a stroke from sharing a straw with a stroke patient. Far more frightening to most people are the causes of amnesia that *are* contagious. Certain viruses or bacteria can infect the brain and cause brain damage so severe that memories are lost.

Such a brain infection is called encephalitis, meaning "swelling of the brain." It can happen when bacteria or viruses enter the brain or the spinal cord. Encephalitis can cause a coma, and it is often deadly. A person who recovers from such an infection may have lasting brain damage, including widespread amnesia.

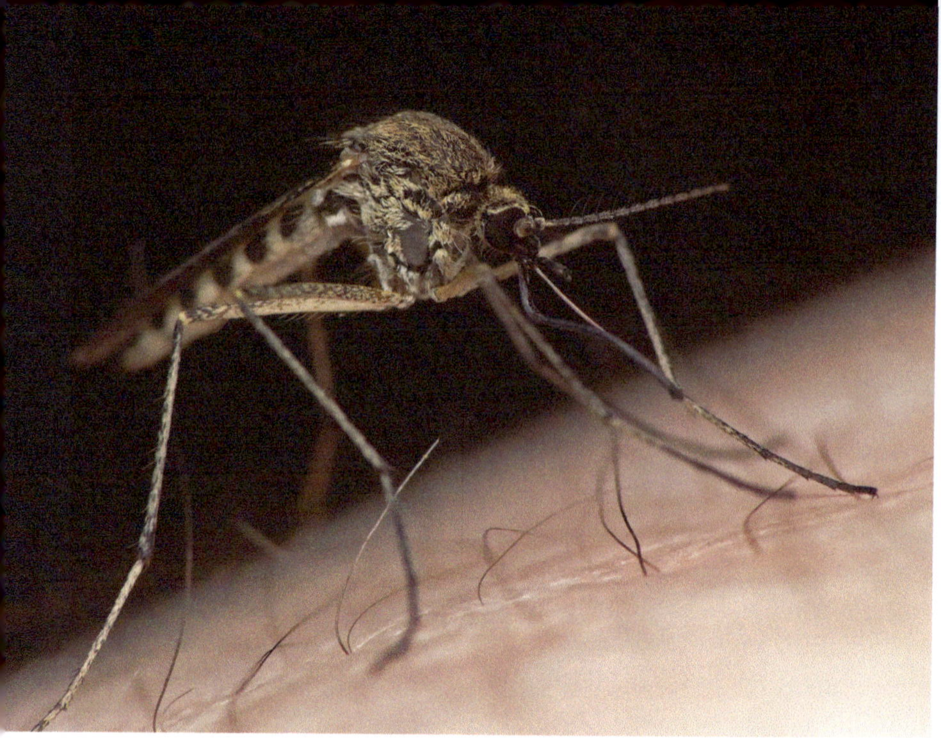

A mosquito carrying the West Nile virus, which can cause brain damage that affects memory, can pass the disease along to humans with its bite.

"Permanent amnesia results from destruction of brain tissue," say Floyd E. Bloom, M. Flint Beal, and David J. Kupfer, authors of *The Dana Guide to Brain Health*. "Such damage can be caused by a variety of mechanisms, including infection."[36]

Quite a few illnesses can lead to encephalitis, and some of the most notorious are carried by insects such as mosquitoes and ticks. Lyme disease and West Nile virus are two examples. Lyme disease is caused by tiny organisms called spirochetes, which are carried by ticks. West Nile virus is carried by mosquitoes. Both insects are parasites that live by sucking the blood of other creatures, including humans. When these pests bite an infected creature, they pick up the virus or bacteria. When next they bite something else, they leave the harmful germs behind. Illnesses such as Lyme disease and West Nile virus can cause serious damage in people, including brain swelling that can destroy memory.

Insects, however, are not the only ones spreading dangerous diseases around. People themselves can pass disease to each other. Common illnesses such as herpes, measles, mumps, and chicken pox can end up in the brain, causing swelling and dangerous damage. Scientists have developed vaccines to prevent many of the illnesses that can be a threat to memory, and fortunately, encephalitis that is serious enough to cause brain damage and amnesia is very rare. When it happens, though, it is life changing.

John E. Douglas, a former agent with the Federal Bureau of Investigation, was helping with a tough case when he came down with viral encephalitis and a fever so high, he says, doctors told his family that "his brain has been fried to a crisp."[37] Douglas was taken to a hospital in the throes of a violent seizure. He spent a week in a coma and had amnesia when he came out of it.

"The recovery was painful and discouraging," he says. "I had to learn to walk again. I was having memory problems." When he went home, he explains, "I'd notice a particular building and not know if it was new. I felt like a stroke victim and wondered if I'd ever be able to work again."[38]

A Shocking Condition

Douglas's infection was in his brain, but an infection anywhere in the body that causes a high fever can also cause a seizure, a rise in the electrical activity in the brain. Seizures, in turn, can damage brain cells necessary for memory.

"Things that irritate the brain, particularly those that irritate a particular part of the brain, can cause neurons to fire erratically,"[39] says Dr. Carl W. Bazil, author of *Living Well with Epilepsy and Other Seizure Disorders*. The result is a seizure.

Seizures can be so mild that they are hardly noticeable. The person just seems to be staring into space for a moment. But seizures can also be severe, causing convulsions, or tensing of muscles in the body. Someone who is having a seizure may begin to jerk uncontrollably and clench his jaw. A major seizure can also cause damage to the brain, and as happened for Douglas, memory loss is one of the possible results.

Few illnesses cause a fever high enough to bring on a seizure and brain damage, but some people have a condition called epilepsy and frequently suffer from minor or major seizures at random. Seizures and epilepsy can be triggered by some of the same things that can cause amnesia.

"Epilepsy most often starts at the extremes of life—in the very young or the very old—although it can begin at any age," says Bazil. "Many things in our lives that affect the brain also have the potential to cause seizures to begin."[40]

A stroke can cause a seizure, for example, and sometimes, a head injury can bring on epilepsy. The famous amnesia patient known as HM, in fact, had surgery on his brain for exactly this reason. When he was nine years old, he suffered a head injury that caused epilepsy. His brain surgery, at age twenty-seven, was supposed to help with the seizures. Unfortunately, it also wiped out his memory, something the seizures themselves had never done.

Solving the Brain's Mysteries

Many of the things that go wrong in the brain that result in brain damage and amnesia are still widely considered to be medical puzzles. However, scientists have been busy developing new technology to study living brains, technology that can create detailed pictures of exactly what is happening in the brain and when. This technology may be the key to preventing some of the causes of amnesia. It may even help doctors to repair brain damage, restore some patients' ability to learn new things again, and perhaps even find the memories that some amnesia patients think are gone forever.

CHAPTER FOUR

Diagnosing Amnesia

In July 2007 a woman wandered the streets of Dallas, Texas, with no destination in mind. She was not familiar with Dallas. In fact, she had no idea how she even got to Dallas. Perhaps she was visiting family or friends. It was also possible that she lived in Dallas. But the woman had no idea where she lived, or even who she was.

Police officers who investigated the situation said the woman was in good health. She simply had no memory. An officer from the Terrell Police Department told CBS News it was the first time he had ever been asked to identify someone with amnesia who just did not know where she was at all.

Situations like this are rare. Most people who have amnesia, or at least their family members, are aware of how they got it in the first place—on the playing field, perhaps, or in a car accident, or, like FBI agent John E. Douglas, after an illness. When a person such as the woman in Dallas is discovered, he or she is usually taken to a hospital in the hope that doctors can unlock the person's memories or at least determine what happened to block them in the first place.

The first step is a general examination. If the person is running a fever, the amnesia could be caused by a brain infection. If the person shows signs of a head injury, such as large pupils in the eyes, this may be what caused the amnesia. Doctors also ask questions to determine how well a person's brain and memory seem to be working as well as what kind of memory loss might be present: retrograde or anteretrograde, depending on whether the person is forgetting old memories or brand-new ones.

"When checking for attention or anteretrograde amnesia," says author and doctor Robert C. Cantu, "useful tests are repeating four words immediately and two minutes later, repeating five numbers forward and especially backward, and repeating the months of the year backward."[41]

Tests like these are often used in situations when amnesia is suspected and there is a need to find out immediately. When a football player suffers a blow to the head during a game, for example, team doctors ask the player certain kinds of questions to test memory. If the player cannot answer them, then he probably has a serious brain injury.

There are better tests to sort out the amount of brain damage and memory loss a person might have suffered. As scientists learn more about how and where the human brain creates and stores memories, they are able to come up with specific kinds of questions that give them clues about what parts of the brain might not be working. These tests take longer than the word-repeat tests a team doctor might use on the playing field, but they also give doctors a more precise picture of what is happening in the brain.

The Wisconsin Card Sorting Test

Since the late 1940s, doctors have been using the Wisconsin Card Sorting Test, or WCST, to see how well a patient's brain is working. The WCST can be used in many situations, and it is one of the common tests a person with amnesia is asked to perform. During the WCST, a doctor places four cards on a table. Each card has a different number of colored shapes on it. The first card, for example, might have one yellow triangle. The second might have two blue squares, and the third might have three red circles. The fourth card might show four green diamonds. The patient is then given a stack of cards that also have colored shapes on them. The task is to compare these cards to the four on the table and sort them into rows.

How the patient does this tells the doctor a lot about how the brain is working. The patient might choose a logical reason for sorting the cards, such as placing the cards in rows by color or placing all pictures of squares in one row and all pictures of circles in another. Many sorting options are possible, but the doctor decides ahead of time on one "correct" way to sort—say, by the number of shapes on the card. As the patient places each new card into a row, the doctor says whether the choice is right or wrong. Most people whose brains work normally, even very young children, can soon figure out the correct way to sort the cards.

"If the subject fails to correctly match the cards according to the unstated guidelines, they must be able to alter their sorting strategy," says Shaheen Emmanuel Lakhan in an article in the *Journal of Medicine*. "Throughout the WCST procedure, the subject is not informed of the reasoning behind the . . . 'right' or 'wrong' feedback."[42]

Doctors examine the process a person uses to arrange the cards and how long it takes him to discover the "right" way to sort them. This information gives doctors some clues about how certain parts of the patient's brain are working.

Language Tests

The ability to use words and language is one of the brain's most important and complicated jobs. Knowing what an object is and being able to describe it in words is simple for someone who has not suffered brain damage, but the process of learning new words and remembering old ones is actually very complicated. A person who has amnesia may not be able to do this very easily. How well a patient uses language, therefore, gives doctors a good idea of how serious memory loss might be.

Physicians Mark Kritchevsky, Judy Chang, and Larry R. Squire describe one patient who came to a San Diego, California, emergency room with a headache and no memory of his name or his past. The last thing he could remember was hitchhiking in some bushes. He had very noticeable problems with language.

"The patient said that he saw the numbers but did not know their names," say Kritchevsky and his colleagues. "He could not name a pen and said that, 'It's to write with.' He could not name a shoe and said that, 'It's to walk on.' He could not name a watch."[43] This man's situation is a good example of how amnesia often causes trouble for a person who is trying to think of words.

Doctors have come up with two good tests of a person's language ability that give a better picture of what parts of the brain have been damaged and how severe a person's memory loss might be. The first test is called the Phonemic Verbal Fluency Test. It is similar to the board game Scattergories: The patient is asked to say or write as many words as she can think of that start with a certain letter. As anyone who has played Scattergories knows, this can take quite a bit of thought, and it depends on certain parts of the brain more than others. A person who struggles with this test will give doctors clues about what part of the brain might have been damaged.

The second language test is called the Stroop Color Word Interference Test. In this test, a person is shown cards with the names of colors on them, printed in black ink. First, the patient reads the words on the cards: for example, *blue*, *red*, and *green*. In the next step of the test, the person is shown cards of differ-

Among the tests given to amnesia patients are those that measure their ability to use language correctly and can thus allow insight to the parts of their brain that are damaged. Patients with memory loss may struggle, for instance, to make a list of words that start with a certain letter.

ent colors and is asked to name the color of each card. In the third step, the patient is shown cards with the names of colors on them, but the words themselves are printed in a different color. For example, a card might have the word *red* written on it, but in green ink. The patient is asked to name the color of the ink, not the word written on the card.

"In the third task," says Lakhan, "the normal tendency to read the words, rather than the color of the ink in which the words are printed, elicits a significant slowing in reaction time (the time it takes to name the correct color)."[44]

Patients who have a long reaction time, or who cannot name the correct color at all but can only read the word, usually have damage in the front part of the brain. This also means they may have problems with memory.

A Need to See the Brain

Language tests and card-sorting tests have been very useful to help doctors discover what parts of a person's brain are not

Take the Stroop Test

How would you do on the Stroop Color Word Interference Test? Try this. Gather felt pens in three different colors of ink: blue, green, and red. On a sheet of white paper, write the words *blue*, *green*, and *red*, but in a different color of ink. For instance, write *blue* in red ink, then *green* in blue ink. Fill the paper with a row of such words. Then, go through the list, saying the color of each word instead of the word itself: If the word *red* is written in green ink, say green, not red. It is harder than it seems. For patients who have had a brain injury, it may be impossible.

This test is often used on people who are climbing Mount Everest, to determine whether the altitude and lack of oxygen are affecting their brains.

working properly, but these tests may do more to satisfy a scientist's curiosity than to help a patient. Just knowing what parts of the brain have suffered the most damage does nothing to cure the patient's amnesia or bring back memories that have disappeared. These tests also do nothing to help doctors see where or how extensive the damage is.

In the 1940s and 1950s, the time period when the Wisconsin Card Sorting Test was invented and when amnesic HM was recovering from his memory-robbing surgery, doctors had no good way to see what was actually happening to a person's brain except by actually cutting into the skull to take a look. Given the risk of complications, the thought of brain surgery is, for most people who have amnesia, more frightening than the memory problems themselves. Brains affected by diseases such as Alzheimer's are best studied after the person has died, when the brain can be removed during an autopsy and examined more closely.

Things are changing, however. Scientists still may not know everything about the brain, but they have come up with brilliant new ways to study it in living patients—without cutting open the skull at all.

The Human Brain, in Pictures

Most great inventions happen by accident, and this was the case in 1895, when a German physicist named Wilhelm Conrad Röntgen happened upon a form of radiation that could make images of the bones underneath the skin of his wife's hand. Röntgen did not know what to call the beams of radiation that did this, so he settled on the letter *X*, to stand for "unknown." The name *X-ray* stuck, and it has been one of the most important medical breakthroughs in all of human history.

X-ray technology has led to many discoveries and has countless uses in medicine. Cracks in broken bones are identified and repaired, bullets from gunshot wounds are found and removed, and cancerous growths are discovered—all through the use of X-rays. Radiation technology makes it possible to do something for which all patients are thankful: Doctors can see what is happening inside the body without having to cut into it.

"Prior to the x-ray, a physician was able to employ only four of the five senses (hearing, smelling, touching, and tasting) in detecting an illness and its causes," say Meyer Friedman and Gerald W. Friedland, authors of *Medicine's 10 Greatest Discoveries*. "Roentgen's discovery allowed the doctor to employ the fifth sense (seeing)—not only for detecting, but often enough for curing a disease."[45]

Nowhere is this more important than the brain. Surgery on this part of the body is extremely difficult. The brain is so well protected that just getting to it is a challenge, and once the brain tissue is exposed, any wrong move by the surgeon could change the patient's life forever.

With the invention of three important types of technology, all of which evolved from X-rays, modern doctors can take very clear pictures of all parts of the brain. They can see where a blood clot has formed in a patient who has had a stroke. They can find swollen areas in a patient with a brain infection. They can examine the damage done by clumping proteins in Alzheimer's disease, and they can see whether new medications for this disease are working. They can also "see" thought processes happening in the brain and find the holes in the pathways of electrical signals that might be causing gaps in memory.

Computed Tomography

X-ray technology has come a long way from the simple, black-and-white pictures doctors use to see if a bone is broken. Computers and X-ray machines now work together to create computed tomography scans, also known as CT or CAT scans, of any part of the body, including soft tissues in the abdomen and the head.

Before CT scans, X-ray pictures were single films showing bones as white areas, soft tissues such as muscles and skin as gray areas, and air as black areas. CT scanning takes similar pictures, but many more of them, to get a better look at an entire part of the body. The pictures of a kidney, for instance,

Drilling for Memories

In the 1940s and 1950s, before there were ways to look at a brain without breaching the skull, about forty thousand lobotomies were performed on patients in the United States. A lobotomy, or surgery on one or more lobes of the brain, was thought to help people with psychiatric disorders. The process was not always surgically safe. Some doctors even used crude drills to perform a lobotomy. Often, the goal was to make aggressive or difficult patients more cooperative, but it usually had the opposite effect. As doctors and patients soon found out, removing or damaging parts of the brain this way can lead to loss of emotions, hostile and rude behavior in social situations, and of course, the loss of memory.

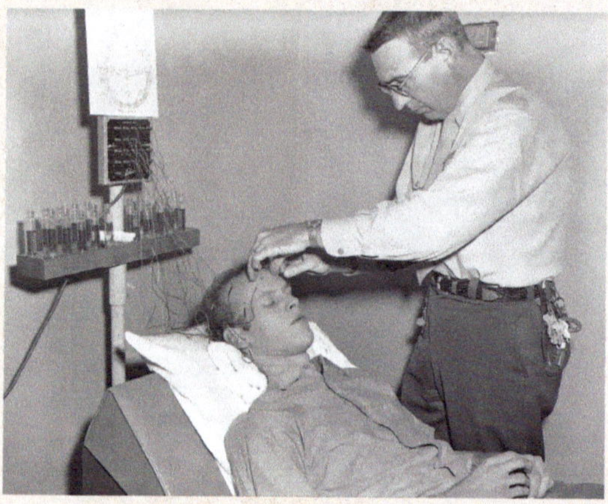

A prisoner is prepped for a lobotomy, a procedure that was once advocated in the mid-20th century as a way to help people overcome psychiatric disorders or curb a person's tendency towards aggressive, hostile, or criminal behavior.

show slices of the organ, almost like cutting a loaf of bread. Separately, each slice shows not only the surface of the kidney but what is beneath it. When the slices are put back together, you see the entire organ again.

CT scanning of the head works much the same way, taking pictures of the skull and brain in slices. A computer then puts the pictures together like a puzzle, so doctors can see a full and detailed picture of the brain, both outside and in. CT scanning of the head helps doctors to find and diagnose many brain problems that might be causing amnesia: Tumors will show up on a CT scan, as will skull fractures and bleeding in the brain if a patient has had a head injury. Blood clots or broken blood vessels that cause strokes can be found quickly on a CT scan, as well. It is a fast, painless way for doctors to find out what might be wiping out a person's memories.

"The CT scan revolutionized neurological diagnosis," say Arthur and Mitchell Bard, authors of *The Complete Idiot's Guide to Understanding the Brain*. "The CT scan eliminated the need for drilling exploratory burr holes in the skill."[46]

Most CT scans of the brain take about twenty minutes. The machine that takes the pictures is called a CT scanner and is shaped like a large donut. The amnesia patient lies on a table,

A doctor may choose to order a CT scan of an amnesia patient's brain, reviewing the series of images in order to identify any problems inside the brain, such as tumors, blood clots, or injuries.

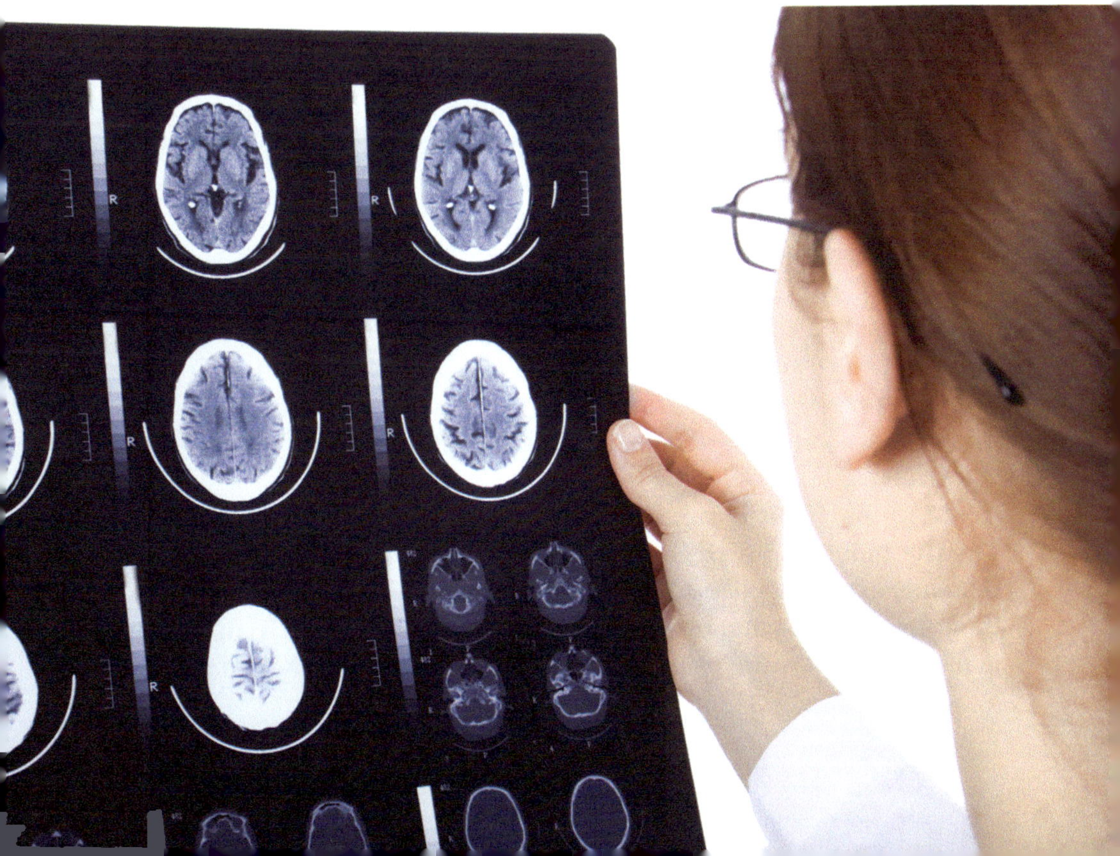

and the table slowly slides through the hole in the center of the machine while pictures are taken.

New CT machines can spin the body around as they take pictures, and this is called a spiral CT. Doctors like these machines because a spiral CT can make three-dimensional pictures of the inside of the body, giving an even better look at brain tissue. Patients like spiral CT machines because they are faster than the older models, so patients do not have to lie perfectly still for quite as long while the machine takes pictures.

Computed tomography is very useful, but it has disadvantages. It exposes patients to radiation, for one thing, so it carries a small risk of causing cancer. CT scans are also a bit better at showing hard tissue, such as the bones of the skull, than showing the details of soft tissue, such as the brain. Doctors working with amnesia patients often use another, newer kind of technology, one that uses magnets instead of X-rays to get a better look at what is beneath the skull.

Magnetic Resonance Imaging

Magnetic resonance imaging, or MRI, takes pictures of the body using magnetic forces. MRI technology provides extremely clear pictures of any type of tissue a doctor wants to look at, even blood flowing in a vein or artery (and perhaps causing memory-blocking damage in the head). MRI scans are used to diagnose many types of diseases, but they are especially useful for looking at the brain.

"An MRI is not bound by the same constrictions as a CT scan," say Richard C. Senelick, Peter W. Rossi, and Karla Dougherty, authors of *Living with Stroke: A Guide for Families*. "It can take pictures of the brain past any skeletal structures; it can depict extraordinary details of specific, minute areas within the brain."[47]

Using magnets to take pictures is very complicated, but like the memory processes it helps to study, MRI technology depends on electrical currents. The body is made up of billions of atoms, the building blocks of cells. Atoms, especially hydrogen atoms, have tiny electrical charges. Magnetic resonance

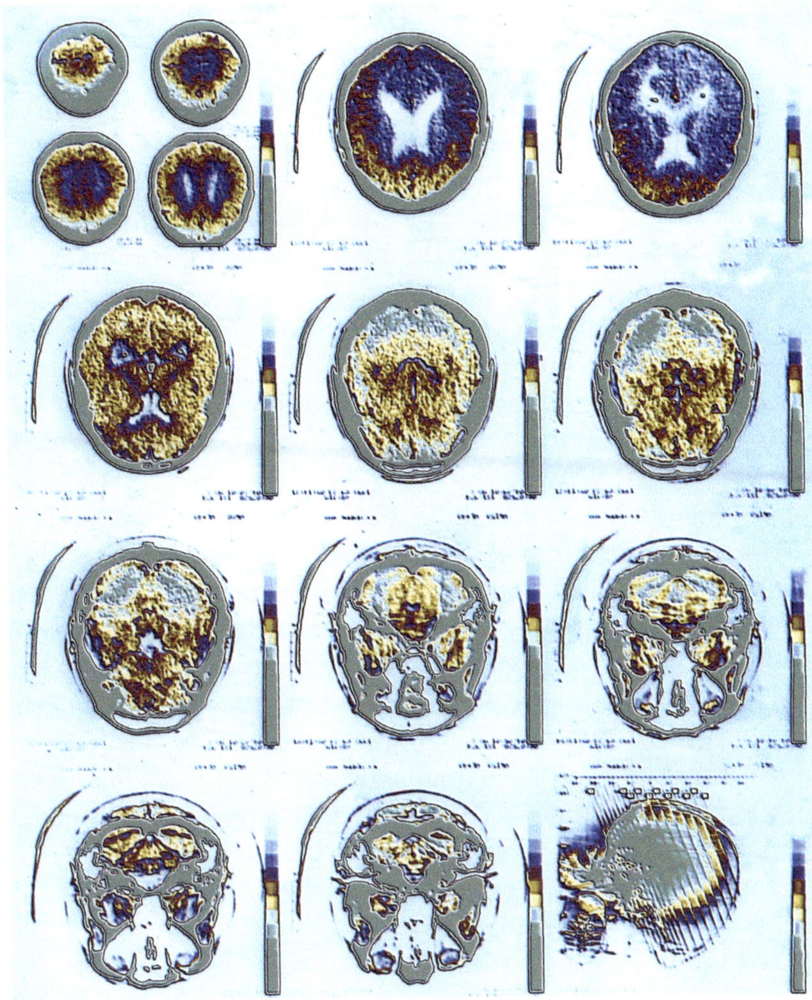

MRI scans provide a view of the brain that is of particular value to doctors looking to diagnose the cause of amnesia.

uses a giant magnet to "spin" these hydrogen atoms, and electrical charges make them line up differently under magnetic forces. Computers are able to read the way the atoms line up and translate the information into pictures of a specific part of the body.

An amnesic patient whose doctor requests an MRI lies on a table, which slides into a long tube. The machine takes pictures of the patient's brain in very thin slices, much like a CT scan. But a CT scan can only take slices from front to back, the way a loaf of bread is sliced. An MRI can take slices in any direction: top to bottom, side to side, even on a diagonal. The "loaves" themselves might look funny this way, but when a computer puts the slices back together, the full image of the brain is clear. So clear, in fact, that it is like looking at the actual brain.

"An MRI can select a point inside the human body and essentially ask it to identify its tissue type," says Tom Philbin in *The 100 Greatest Inventions of All Time: A Ranking Past to Present*. The MRI, he says, can "'look' at the soft tissues of the body. The brain, spinal cord, and nerves in particular are seen much more clearly with an MRI."[48]

MRI technology is still quite new, but it is the best method doctors have for looking at the kinds of brain problems that cause amnesia. Most importantly, MRI images of the brain can even be taken while a patient looks at a certain type of picture or does other tasks. These images can help doctors see what parts of the brain are working at different times and what parts are not. With technology such as this, scientists are able to learn much more about how the brain works and the particular parts of it that cause amnesia. Someday, this might make surgical repair of the brain possible to reconnect an amnesiac's memory.

Electroencephalogram

Seeing the activity of a working brain depends on reading the electrical pulses that neurons are constantly sending back and forth, even when we are asleep. Brain cells talk to each other by way of electrical charges. Therefore, it is possible to measure the electrical activity in the brain to figure out what parts are communicating and what is not working properly. An electroencephalogram, or EEG, is a test doctors use to eavesdrop on what brain cells are telling each other. The "gram" part of the process is a sheet of paper with wavy lines on it, showing doctors the pattern of the electrical activity that is happening in the brain.

During an EEG, flat, metal discs called electrodes are stuck all over the patient's scalp. Each of these electrodes has a wire that connects it to the recording machine, which draws the

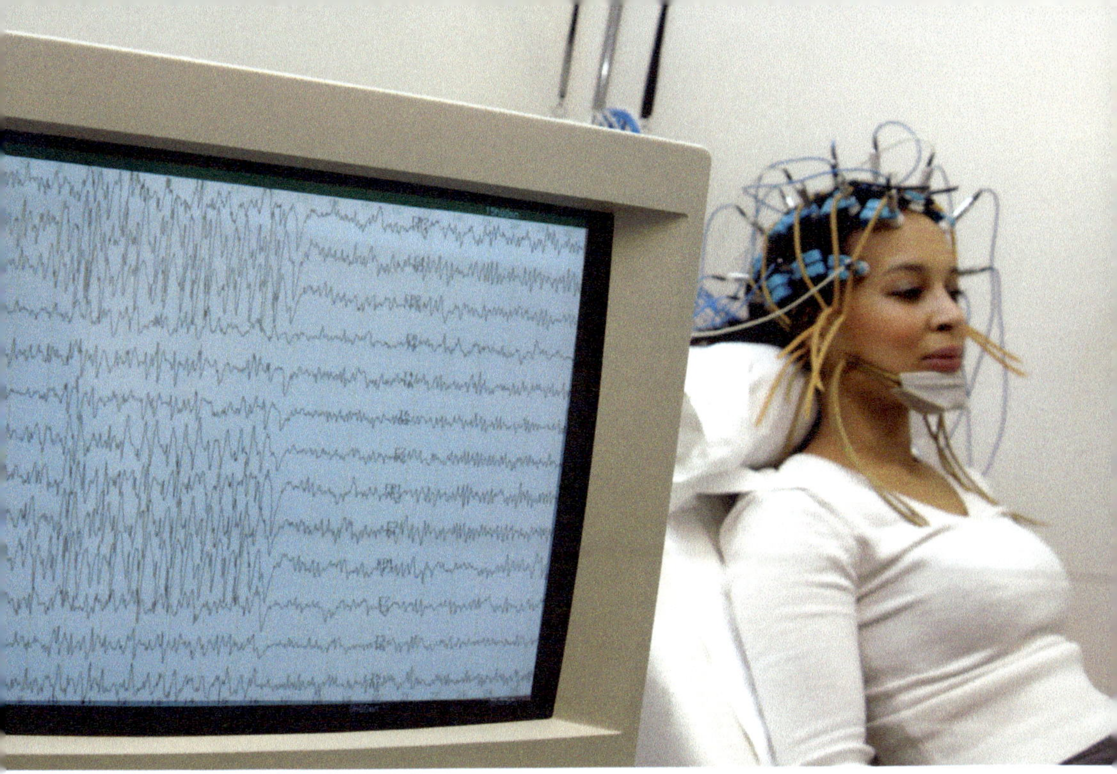

A woman undergoes an EEG to monitor the electrical activity of her brain, which is represented in the graphs on the computer screen.

lines of the graph. The electrodes look and feel strange, but the process is not painful. They pick up the signals that are jumping around deep beneath the skull.

EEGs can help doctors see how brain cells are communicating and how the brain is responding to senses such as sight and hearing. The graph may seem like nothing but a series of wiggly lines to the untrained eye, but brain specialists can use it to learn more about all kinds of brain conditions, even attention deficit disorder (ADD), sleeping problems, and hallucinations (when the patient "sees" things that are not there). EEGs are also used for patients who are in a coma to see if there is still any activity going on in the brain. The EEG may be one of the keys to unlocking some of the mysteries surrounding memory loss.

Paired with other tests such as CT scans and MRIs, EEGs provide important clues about what is happening inside a person's brain to cause memory problems. As these kinds of technology evolve and become more sensitive and detailed than ever before, they give hope to thousands of people who live with memory loss. One day, there may be a way to "recharge" a sick or injured brain and dig up memories that have been buried. For now, however, there still is no cure for amnesia. People with the condition can only take part in imaging tests such as CT and MRI scans and hope to make history as part of a future cure for memory problems.

CHAPTER FIVE

Treating Memory Loss

London resident Clive Wearing's memory is exactly seven seconds long. Anything he learns or sees or does is forgotten in the amount of time it would take him to read this sentence. But Wearing's life was not always this way. There was a time when he was one of the world's greatest musicians. He directed a world-famous London symphony and even created the music played at the wedding of England's Prince Charles and Princess Diana. Then, in March 1985, he came down with encephalitis. The herpes virus, the same germ that causes common cold sores, found its way into his brain and created a life-threatening infection.

Encephalitis cases such as Wearing's are very rare but very serious. Seven out of ten people who get herpes encephalitis die if it is not treated immediately. Wearing did not die, but his memory did. The infection attacked the main memory centers of his brain. He recovered from the illness, but he has never recovered his memories. He lives with what experts believe is the worst case of amnesia in known history.

Wearing remembers nothing from before his illness, and he has remembered nothing since. He can still speak, but every day, he greets his wife as if meeting her for the very first time. Sometimes he asks if she is the queen of England. Amazingly, though, Wearing can still play melodies. Beautifully.

"Though he could no longer read books or a newspaper," says Jan Goodwin in an article in *Reader's Digest*, "Clive, it turned out, could still read music." The ability to play music, like the ability to speak or ride a bike, is part of a person's procedural memory—not the memory of facts such as names and faces, but of processes. All of Wearing's new memories melt away in seconds. But he sits down at a piano, says Goodwin, "and sounds extremely accomplished."[49]

Memory Training

Thankfully, few people with amnesia have cases as serious as those of HM in the 1950s and Wearing in the 1980s. Most people lose only some of their memories. With the help of simple memory techniques and everyday tools such as sticky notes, date books, and alarm features on cell phones, they can remember what they need to know to get through a day.

"Depending on the degree of amnesia and its cause, victims may be able to lead relatively normal lives," says Julia Barrett in the *Encyclopedia of Medicine*. "Amnesiacs can learn through therapy to rely on other memory systems to compensate for what is lost."[50]

People with amnesia may rely on reminder lists and other memory tools to help them manage daily life.

Memory therapy is a form of amnesia treatment that helps some people relearn how to remember. This treatment is similar to what students call study skills, ways to improve the ability to memorize information. One useful technique in memory therapy is mnemonics, a memory trick that dates back to the time of the ancient Greeks. People use mnemonics to recall lists of things, such as items to buy at the grocery store. If the list includes milk, oranges, and potato chips, a mnemonic might take the first letter of each item to make the word *mop*. The shopper can then remember that the list has three items, and what they are, just by remembering the word *mop*, or even just the image of one. Training people with anteretrograde amnesia to use such methods can make it easier for them to live with their memory difficulties.

"Remembering is a process that must be learned, just like walking, talking, eating," says Tanushree Podder, author of the book *Smart Memory*. "You learned these things when you were a child and now you can perform them without effort."[51] According to Podder, the memory process is an example of implicit learning, the kind of learning that, like riding a bicycle, rarely disappears with amnesia. "You can learn the process of using your memory just as thoroughly," she says. "Anyone can hone up the memory by training it."[52]

Training people with memory problems to use mnemonics and other memory tricks is one of the best forms of treatment for the types of amnesia that affect the ability to learn new information. Memory therapy is not a cure for amnesia, however, and it does not repair the damage that has been done to the brain. It also provides little help for people with retrograde amnesia, who have lost past memories that no amount of training and relearning will bring back.

In desperation, some people with retrograde amnesia try other ways to unlock the memories they cannot reach. Doing so is often controversial. Probably the most popular method, and certainly the most notorious, is hypnosis.

Forgetful, or a Fraud?

In 2003 a stockbroker named Doug Bruce lost his memory and wound up on a New York City subway. The story of his memory loss and his struggle to rebuild his life is told in the 2006 documentary film, *Unknown White Male*.

Some people think the film is a hoax. It states that Bruce's identity troubles were featured in the news before his family was eventually tracked down, but critics of the film say no such news story or newspaper article can be found. They also say it is a little too convenient that that the man who directed the film, Rupert Murray, just happens to be a longtime friend of Bruce (even though he, like Bruce these days, cannot remember exactly how or where they met).

Unknown White Male is a story of a life without the benefit of a memory. It is hard to imagine someone pretending to act that way for the rest of his life just to gain fame in a documentary. Even the film's critics admit that it is either one of the most convincing hoaxes of all time, or the story is real.

Hypnosis

In a psychotherapist's view, hypnosis is a method of changing a person's state of mind. When people are hypnotized, they are somewhere between being asleep and being awake. They do not know where they are or what is around them. The person doing the hypnotizing can suggest certain things, and the person being hypnotized will usually do them.

Some people are more easily hypnotized than others, but scientists think everyone can be hypnotized at least a little. In a hypnotic state, a person can be talked into certain things and talked out of others. A magician might use hypnotism during a show to make a volunteer croak like a frog or waddle around the stage like a duck, but hypnotists also have more serious jobs. Many doctors use hypnotism to help patients with pain from things like headaches, serious burns, and childbirth. Hypnotists also help people to break bad habits such as smoking or to overcome illnesses such as depression.

It makes sense that someone with amnesia might look to hypnotism to find lost memories. After all, hypnotism itself can cause amnesia. If the hypnotist tells the patient that she will remember nothing that happens while she is hypnotized, she will "wake up" with no memory of waddling like a duck. (Unfortunately for her, the brain does make memories of things that happen during hypnosis, so the hypnotist, by saying a certain word or giving a certain cue, can usually make her remember the whole embarrassing event.)

Even psychologist Sigmund Freud tried to use hypnosis to help troubled patients, whom he called hysterics, to track down memories of frightening experiences from their

A young patient submits to hypnotherapy, a controversial method used by some people attempting to retrieve lost or repressed memories.

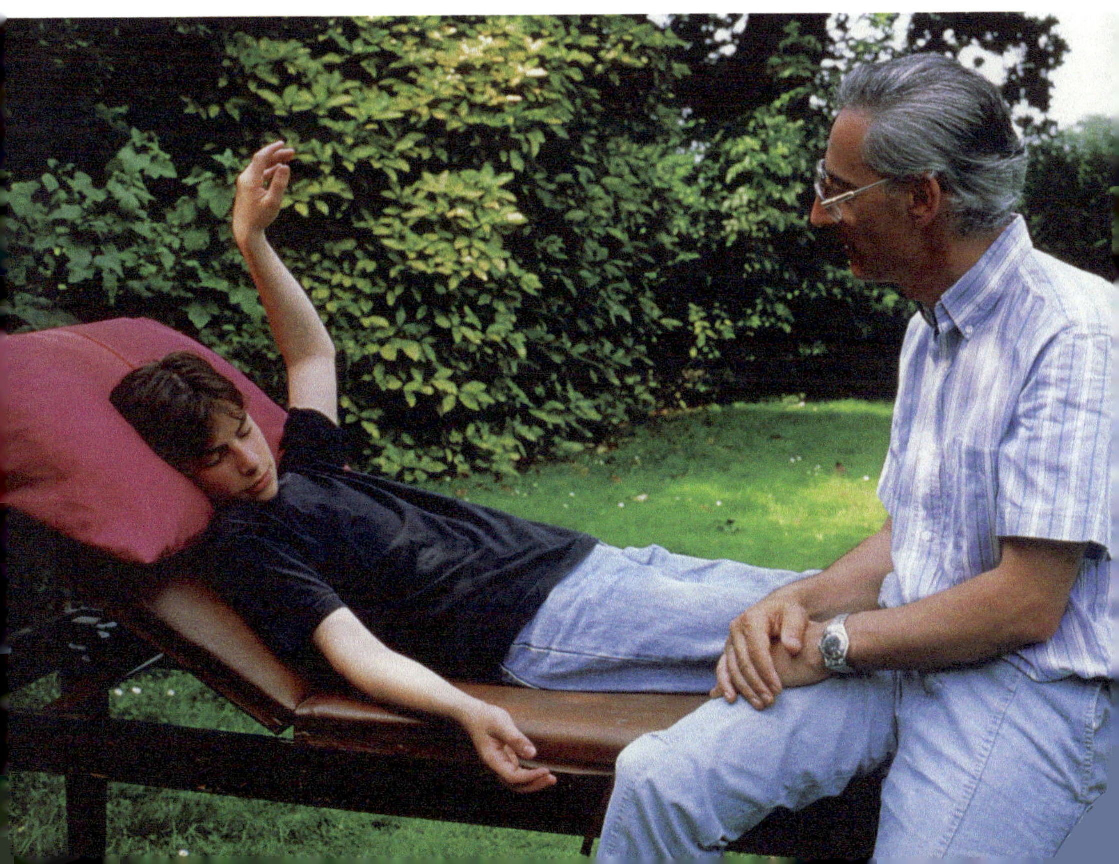

childhood. "Hysterics," he said, "suffer for the most part from reminiscences."[53]

The trouble with using hypnosis to "find" memories is that the memories an amnesiac gets back may not have existed in the first place. A woman may be missing her memory of the entire period from age three through six and may turn to hypnosis because she worries that some troubling event, such as child abuse, caused her mind to shut down and block terrible memories from that age. But it is difficult for a hypnotized adult to tap into memories that happened when she was three. Adults still think like adults, and three-year-olds think like three-year-olds. What the woman "remembers" under hypnosis might only be what she imagines she might have thought and remembered at that age. Worse yet, it might be what the hypnotist makes her believe might have happened.

"Age regression is first and foremost a product of the imagination," says John F. Kihlstrom, a psychology professor at the University of California, Berkeley. "Any accurate memory produced is likely to be blended with a great deal of false recall."[54]

Hypnosis, then, is not necessarily the answer to amnesia. In fact, many memory experts think that memories recalled during hypnosis may not be true memories at all.

"Hypnosis, alas, is not a truth serum," says Dr. Roberta Temes. "More unfortunately, hypnosis *is* a confidence builder. This means that when hypnotized you remember an incident which may or may not have actually occurred, and hypnosis will make you feel confident that your memory is correct and that it did occur."[55]

Kihlstrom says that because so many patients, when hypnotized, actually remember false information, "the risks of distortion vastly outweigh the chances of obtaining any useful information."[56] In short, hypnosis is not the miracle cure a person with amnesia may be hoping for. There is, in fact, no reliable cure for this condition. So far, modern medicine's best hope for battling amnesia is preventing the things that cause it in the first place.

Healthy Lifestyle: A Memory Backup

Amnesia is not an illness in itself, but one of the possible effects of many illnesses and injuries. Scientists may not have found a way to cure amnesia, but every day, they are finding more ways to prevent it. One of the best ways people can protect themselves is simply by doing things that are good for the brain. There is evidence that even Alzheimer's disease, the cause of which is not entirely understood, might be headed off by

Keeping active and exercising regularly is a key factor in maintaining a healthy lifestyle, which may lower the risk of developing medical conditions that can lead to memory loss.

healthy living. Simple habits such as eating nutritious foods, getting plenty of exercise, and keeping the mind active with lifelong learning have been shown to lower the risks. A healthy lifestyle can also help prevent strokes, another common and unforgiving thief of memory.

"There is no specific medical treatment to help reverse the memory loss that occurs after a stroke," says Dr. Alberto Maud. "The best way to prevent dementia after stroke is to avoid having a stroke."[57]

Keeping clear blood vessels, and thus, clear memories begins with a low-fat diet and plenty of exercise. It also means not smoking or abusing alcohol. The sooner a healthy lifestyle begins, doctors agree, the better the odds that the brain will never be damaged and memories will forever remain safely stored. Healthy habits are an important investment in a person's memory bank.

A Helmet for the Mind

Healthy living involves an active lifestyle, but ironically, this too can cause amnesia if a person plays contact sports or has other hobbies that can be risky for the head. For every per-

Bicycle riders can reduce their risk of sustaining a traumatic brain injury in a fall or accident by wearing a helmet.

son in the United States having a stroke right now, two people are hurting their heads on sports fields, bicycles, halfpipes, or roller blades. Every twenty seconds, someone in the United States gets a brain injury, and many of these people, after being knocked unconscious, have posttraumatic amnesia—memory loss that results from an injury to the brain.

Strokes and other memory-robbing diseases usually do their work later in life. Traumatic brain injury, on the other hand, is the most likely cause of amnesia in kids, teens, and young adults. Head-harming accidents are responsible for most of the memories lost in people who are young. Professionals in the field of athletics are among those helping to make more people aware of the dangers of head injury.

"Team physicians, athletic trainers, and other medical personnel responsible for the medical care of athletes face no more challenging problem than the recognition and management of concussion," says author and doctor Robert C. Cantu. "Such injuries have captured many headlines in recent years and have spurred studies within both the National Football League and the National Hockey League."[58]

Preventing traumatic brain injury takes a combination of technology and common sense. Simply remembering to put on a helmet before climbing on a bicycle or to buckle a seat belt in the car could prevent a serious, life-changing brain injury.

"In children, brain injuries usually result from motor vehicle or sports accidents, or from falls," says author Lisa Schoenbrodt. "These events tend to create violent movement of the brain within a closed skull."[59]

Traumatic brain injuries can do more harm to the brain than almost any other cause of amnesia. According to On With Life, an Iowa-based nonprofit organization providing brain-injury rehabilitation services, posttraumatic amnesia usually gets better after a few days, weeks, or months. In the meantime, however, those who know the person may feel puzzled by his or her inability to remember things from day to day or hour to hour.

Survivors of serious brain injury may also be embarrassed during this period of amnesia. Amnesia sufferer Jill Robinson writes, "How many of these questions did I ask yesterday, and how many have already been answered?"[60]

Living with Lost Memories

Life with amnesia is very difficult, not just for the person with memory loss but for friends and family, who may feel as if they are strangers to someone they love. Even if memory loss only affects short-term memory, life is no picnic. A person with short-term memory loss remembers friends and family, as well as most of the important details of his life. But if someone asks him to go to the store for a carton of milk, he not only forgets the milk, but he may also forget to go to the store at all and could wind up someplace else entirely.

Mnemonics and other memory-training techniques can be helpful, but even so, learning anything new takes a lot of time and effort for someone with short-term memory loss. Studying for a test at school might take most kids an hour, but a student with amnesia could spend days trying to memorize the same facts (and still do poorly on the test). Sadly, once memories or the ability to remember are gone, they may be gone for good.

Medical staff prepare a patient for electroconvulsive shock therapy, which is sometimes used to treat patients with severe depression. However, the treatment can have the side effect of inducing amnesia.

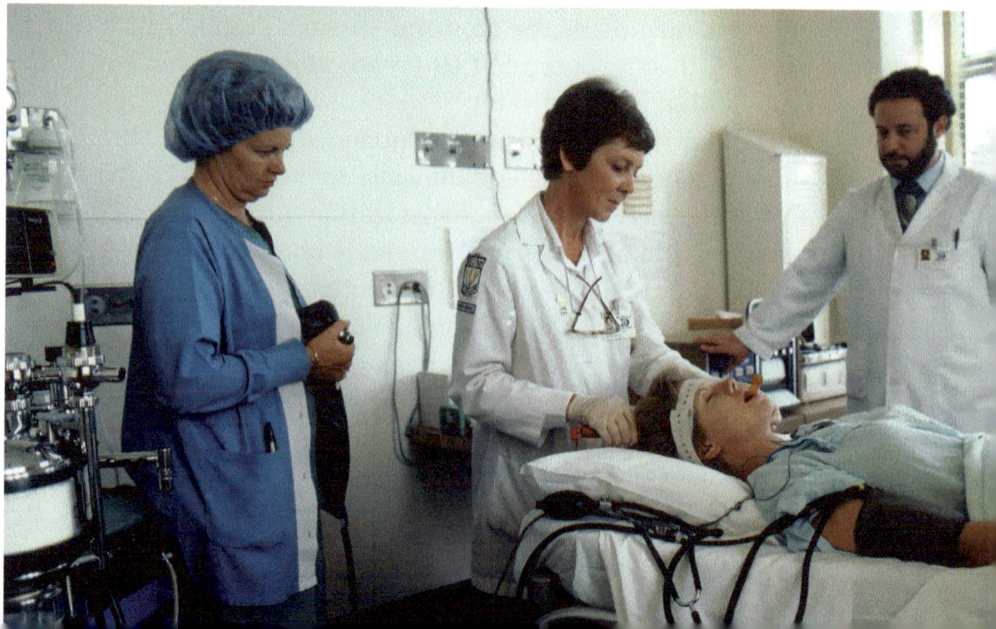

Time occasionally fixes things and puts memories back where they belong, but doctors have found no cure for amnesia.

There is no pill someone can take that will bring back lost memories. How the brain works is still so poorly understood that doctors have a hard time figuring out just what goes on in the brain to create memories or to lose them, much less what kind of medications could repair the many types of brain damage that can lead to amnesia. In fact, some medications and treatments that have been used for mental disorders such as depression have in turn caused amnesia.

Electroconvulsive shock therapy is one such example. This treatment, which is sometimes used for people who suffer from very severe depression, involves having electrodes attached to the temples of the head so that mild electric shocks can be applied to the brain. The goal of this therapy is to reset circuits in the brain that might not be working properly, which scientists believe may cause depression. One common side effect of shock therapy, however, is mild amnesia that lasts for hours or even days. Because electroconvulsive shock therapy usually requires many treatments, some scientists believe that the repeated shock sessions may lead to long-term amnesia.

"Electroconvulsive therapy is actually one of the safest and most effective treatments for severe depression," say neuroscience researchers Mary H. Kosmidis and Andrew C. Papanicolaou, but they point out concerns about this treatment that come from its link to amnesia and its "potential for causing permanent brain damage."[61]

The risks involved with treatments such as electroshock therapy are evidence that scientists still have a great deal to learn about the human brain. Experimenting with new treatments for amnesia might mean causing even more damage to an injured brain. The lessons learned from cases such as the epilepsy treatment of HM make doctors and scientists wary of trying to treat amnesia with medications or surgery. For now, most people who have amnesia must simply learn to live with it the best they can.

Life with Amnesia

Perhaps the hardest part of living with amnesia is that so many people do not understand this condition. TV and Hollywood often portray the disorder to be much different than it actually is.

"Real, diagnosable amnesia—people getting knocked on the head and forgetting their names—is a rare condition, and usually a brief one," says Jonathan Lethem, editor of *The Vintage Book of Amnesia: An Anthology of Writing on the Subject of Memory Loss.* "In books and movies, though, versions of amnesia lurk everywhere. Amnesiacs might not much exist, but amnesiac characters stumble everywhere through comic books, movies, and our dreams."[62]

Clinical neuropsychologist Sallie Baxendale says, "In most films, memories are not lost, just made temporarily inaccessible. Recovery of memory is possible, via various unlikely means."[63] In reality, however, as most people who work or live with amnesia know, memories can hide and never be found. The brain is an incredibly complicated thing, and reaching in after foggy memories often means coming up empty-handed. Living with amnesia requires a great deal of patience on the part of the amnesiac as well as his or her family and friends.

Gentle, frequent reminders may be the best help yet for amnesia of all kinds. A person who cannot remember names and faces or what day of the week it is may simply need kind reminders of these things. Friends and family members of people who have Alzheimer's disease learn not to be offended if their loved one forgets their name or cannot remember important events such as birthdays, and the same patience and kindness can help anyone whose memory has been damaged by injury or disease. Helping someone with retrograde memory loss, the absence of memories from a period of time in the past, might mean sharing pictures and stories of the times that have been forgotten. Unlike the cases of amnesia in movies and television shows, these activities and reminders probably will not

Patients with retrograde memory loss may use photos and stories as reminders of events and people from times they can no longer recall.

bring lost memories back in a sudden, joyous flood. However, they might help the amnesia patient to make sense of life with lost memories.

Hoping for a Cure

Current medicine offers little promise for people who have lost their ability to remember things, but even as some brains bury memories, other brains are inventing new technology that brings science closer to finding them. New methods for taking pictures of the brain and for mapping its activity have given brain researchers the tools they need to continue learning how this mysterious organ, the most complicated in the human body, works. The more scientists know about the brain, the closer they get to repairing the damage caused by illnesses, injury, and psychologically disturbing events that have the power to destroy memory.

Amnesia in Hollywood

Too many movies to count feature characters with some kind of impaired memory. Popular movies like *50 First Dates* and *Santa Who?* show a funny side of what life might be like with a memory glitch. In *Men in Black*, agents wipe out people's memories on purpose to protect them from nightmarish recollections of aliens that walk in disguise among us.

The idea of putting forgetful characters in leading movie roles is nothing new. At least ten of the silent movies made before 1926 had this theme, and screenwriters have never tired of it. But in real life, amnesia does not always make a good story, and it rarely goes away just in time for a happy ending. Perhaps one of the most true-to-life amnesic characters to hit the big screen did so in the animated film *Finding Nemo*. The absent-minded fish, Dory, cannot learn new things or remember where she is going. This everyday forgetfulness is perhaps much closer to the reality of life with amnesia than the daring, heroic stunts Jason Bourne pulls off in *The Bourne Identity*, even without knowing how he learned them.

Extreme cases of amnesia are often portrayed in movies and television, with great dramatic or comedic effect. Nemo's forgetful but funny friend Dory, right, from the 2003 Disney movie *Finding Nemo*, is one of many characters with amnesia that have come out of Hollywood.

The loss of memory is not life threatening, but it is certainly life-changing. Amnesia patients and their loved ones have little choice but to hope for a miracle, a key to the memory abilities locked away in their brains. Science currently offers these people very little hope, but one day, doctors may learn enough about the brain to find a cure for lost memories, giving back to amnesiacs their past—and their future.

Notes

Chapter 1: How the Brain Makes Memories

1. Eric R. Kandel, *In Search of Memory: The Emergence of a New Science of Mind*. New York: Norton, 2006, p. xii.
2. Lisa Schoenbrodt, *Children with Traumatic Brain Injury: A Parent's Guide*. Bethesda, MD: Woodbine House, 2001, p. 137.
3. Kandel, *In Search of Memory*, p. xi.
4. Kandel, *In Search of Memory*, p. xii.
5. James S. Nairne, *Psychology: The Adaptive Mind*, 4th ed. Belmont, CA: Wadsworth, 2005, p. 77.
6. Daniel L. Schacter, *Searching for Memory: The Brain, the Mind, and the Past*. New York: Basic Books, 1997, p. 144.
7. Diane Ackerman, *An Alchemy of Mind: The Marvel and Mystery of the Brain*. New York: Scribner, 2004, p. 37.
8. Schacter, *Searching for Memory*, p. 147.
9. Nairne, *Psychology*, p. 61.
10. Schoenbrodt, *Children with Traumatic Brain Injury*, p. 144.
11. Richard M. Restak, *The Modular Brain: How New Discoveries in Neuroscience Are Answering Age-Old Questions About Memory, Free Will, Consciousness and Personal Identity*. New York: Lisa Drew, 1994, p. 78.

Chapter 2: What Is Amnesia?

12. Quoted in "Amnesia Victim Rescue," *Jet*, February 28, 2005, available at http://findarticles.com/p/articles/mi_m1355/is_/ai_n11834087?tag=artBody;col1.
13. Robert W. Howard, *Learning and Memory: Major Ideas, Principles, Issues and Applications*. Westport, CT: Praeger, 1995, p. 8.

14. Nairne, *Psychology*, p. 289.
15. Howard, *Learning and Memory*, p. 64.
16. Howard, *Learning and Memory*, p. 64.
17. Schacter, *Searching for Memory*, p. 138.
18. Schacter, *Searching for Memory*, p. 154.
19. Jill Robinson, *Past Forgetting: My Memory Lost and Found*. New York: Cliff Street, 1999, p. 6.
20. Mayo Clinic Staff, "Transient Global Amnesia," MayoClinic.com, www.mayoclinic.com/health/transient-global-amnesia/DS01022/DSECTION=2.
21. Mayo Clinic Staff, "Transient Global Amnesia."
22. Martin T. Orne, Wayne G. Whitehouse, David F. Dinges, and Emily Carota Orne, "Reconstructing Memory Through Hypnosis: Forensic and Clinical Applications," in *Hypnosis and Memory*, ed. Helen M. Pettinati. New York: Guilford, 1988, p. 32.
23. Theodore G. Brna, Jr., "Psychogenic Amnesia," *American Family Physician*, January 1990, http://findarticles.com/p/articles/mi_m3225/is_/ai_8773339.
24. Quoted in Restak, *The Modular Brain*, p. 93.

Chapter 3: What Causes Amnesia?

25. Schoenbrodt, *Coping with Mild Traumatic Brain Injury*, p. 150.
26. Temple Grandin and Catherine Johnson, *Animals in Translation: Using the Mysteries of Autism to Decode Animal Behavior*. New York: Scribner, 2005, p. 55.
27. Robert C. Cantu, "Posttraumatic Retrograde and Anteretrograde Amnesia: Pathophysiology and Implications in Grading and Safe Return to Play," *Journal of Athletic Training* 36, 2001, pp. 244–48.
28. Cantu, "Posttraumatic Retrograde and Anteretrograde Amnesia," p. 245.
29. Sandra J. Judd, *Brain Disorders Sourcebook*. Detroit: Omnigraphics, 2005, p. 217.
30. Judd, *Brain Disorders Sourcebook*, p. 207.
31. Alberto Maud, "Memory Loss After Stroke," *Neurology* 67, 2006, pp. 14–15.

32. Thomas DeBaggio, *Losing My Mind: An Intimate Look at Life with Alzheimer's*. New York: Free Press, 2003, p. 207.
33. Maud, "Memory Loss After Stroke," p. 15.
34. Lawrence H. Wyatt, "Stroke: Know What to Do," *Journal of the American Chiropractic Association*, August 2004, http://findarticles.com/p/articles/mi_qa3841/is_200408/ai_n9453066/pg_1.
35. Schacter, *Searching for Memory*, p. 145.
36. Floyd E. Bloom, M. Flint Beal, and David J. Kupfer, *The Dana Guide to Brain Health*. New York: Free Press, 2003, p. 636.
37. John E. Douglas and Mark Olshaker, *Mindhunter*. New York: Scribner, 1995, p. 20.
38. Douglas and Olshaker, *Mindhunter*, pp. 21–22.
39. Carl W. Bazil, *Living Well with Epilepsy and Other Seizure Disorders*. New York: HarperCollins, 2004, p. 34.
40. Bazil, *Living Well with Epilepsy and Other Seizure Disorders*, p. 38.

Chapter 4: Diagnosing Amnesia

41. Cantu, "Posttraumatic Retrograde and Anteretrograde Amnesia," p. 245.
42. Shaheen Emmanuel Lakhan, "Neuropsychological Generation of Source Amnesia," *Journal of Medicine* 1, 2007, www.scientificjournals.org/journals2007/articles/1038.htm.
43. Mark Kritchevsky, Judy Chang, and Larry R. Squire, "Functional Amnesia: Clinical Description and Neuropsychological Profile of 10 Cases," *Learning & Memory* 11, 2004, pp. 213–226.
44. Lakhan, "Neuropsychological Generation of Source Amnesia."
45. Meyer Friedman and Gerald W. Friedland, *Medicine's 10 Greatest Discoveries*. New Haven, CT: Yale University Press, 1998, p. 130.
46. Arthur Bard and Mitchell Bard, *The Complete Idiot's Guide to Understanding the Brain*. Indianapolis, IN: Al-

pha, 2002, p. 275.

47. Richard C. Senelick, Peter W. Rossi, and Karla Dougherty, *Living with Stroke: A Guide for Families: Help and New Hope for All Those Touched by Stroke*. Chicago: Contemporary, 1999, p. 94.
48. Tom Philbin, *The 100 Greatest Inventions of All Time: A Ranking Past to Present*. New York: Citadel, 2005, p. 157.

Chapter 5: Treating Memory Loss

49. Jan Goodwin, "Forget Me Not," *Reader's Digest*, June 2006, www.rd.com/stories/inspiration/amnesia-story/article.html.
50. Julia Barrett, "Amnesia," in *Gale Encyclopedia of Medicine*. Detroit: Gale, 1999, http://findarticles.com/p/articles/mi_g2601/is_0000/ai_2601000059.
51. Tanushree Podder, *Smart Memory: Techniques to Improve Memory*. New Delhi: Pustak Mahal, 2005, p. 10.
52. Podder, *Smart Memory*, p. 10.
53. Sigmund Freud and Josef Breuer, *Studies in Hysteria*. London: Penguin, 2004, p. 222.
54. John F. Kihlstrom, "Hypnosis, Memory and Amnesia," *Philosophical Transactions of the Royal Society B: Biological Sciences* 352, 1997, pp. 1727–32.
55. Roberta Temes, *The Complete Idiot's Guide to Hypnosis*. Indianapolis, IN: Alpha, 1999, p. 314.
56. Kihlstrom, "Hypnosis, Memory and Amnesia," p. 1731.
57. Maud, "Memory Loss After Stroke," p. 15.
58. Cantu, "Posttraumatic Retrograde and Anteretrograde Amnesia," p. 245.
59. Schoenbrodt, *Children with Traumatic Brain Injury*, p. 139.
60. Robinson, *Past Forgetting*, p. 50.
61. Mary H. Kosmidis and Andrew C. Papanicolaou, "Electroconvulsive Therapy–Induced Amnesia," in *The Amnesias: A Clinical Textbook of Memory Disorders*, ed. Andrew C. Papanicolaou. New York: Oxford University Press, 2006, p. 204.

62. Jonathan Lethem, ed., *The Vintage Book of Amnesia: An Anthology of Writing on the Subject of Memory Loss.* New York: Vintage, 2000, p. xiii.
63. Sallie Baxendale, "Memories Aren't Made of This: Amnesia at the Movies," *British Medical Journal* 329, 2004, pp. 1480–83.

Glossary

Alzheimer's disease: A brain disease that causes memory loss and impaired thinking.

amnesia: Loss of memory, usually brought on by brain illness or injury.

anteretrograde amnesia: The inability to form new memories after the onset of amnesia.

axon: The part of a nerve cell that sends electrical signals to other cells.

brain stem: The part of the brain that connects to the spinal cord.

cerebrovascular accident (CVA): See *stroke*.

cerebrum: The top and front portion of the brain, believed to be responsible for thought and memory.

coma: Deep unconsciousness, usually caused by injury or disease.

computed tomography (CT): A three-dimensional X-ray in which pictures of an organ are taken in cross-sections, or slices.

declarative memory: See *explicit memory*.

dendrite: The part of a nerve cell that receives electrical signals from other cells.

electrode: The discs placed on a person's scalp during an electroencephalogram to conduct an electrical current.

electroencephalogram (EEG): A test that records brain waves and patterns of brain activity.

encephalitis: Swelling of the brain.

epilepsy: A brain disorder in which abnormal electrical activity causes brief periods of unconsciousness or convulsions.

explicit memory: Memory for facts and information.

forebrain: One of the three main divisions of the brain, responsible for processing information and making choices.

frontal lobe: The front lobe, or portion, of each hemisphere of the brain.

herpes virus: A virus that causes skin blisters and can move to the brain to cause encephalitis.

hindbrain: One of the three main divisions of the brain, mainly responsible for bodily functions that do not require thought.

hippocampus: A structure of the brain believed to be involved in forming, storing, and processing memories.

hypnosis: A trance or sleeplike state brought on by a person making hypnotic suggestions.

implicit memory: Memory for processes; memory for how to do things.

Korsakoff's psychosis: See *Wernicke-Korsakoff syndrome.*

long-term memory: Memory that is stored in the brain for a long time, often permanently.

Lyme disease: An illness, carried by ticks, that can cause neurological disorders such as memory loss.

magnetic resonance imaging (MRI): The use of sound waves and magnets to create three-dimensional, computerized images of an organ in the body.

midbrain: One of the three main divisions of the brain, responsible for many higher-level brain functions.

mnemonic: A tool or task that aids memory.

neuron: A nerve cell, made of a cell body, dendrites, and axons; a building block of brain tissue.

occipital lobe: The lobe of each hemisphere of the brain that is responsible for vision.

parietal lobe: The lobe of each hemisphere of the brain that is responsible for processing body sensations.

Phonemic Verbal Fluency Test: A test used to evaluate brain function in which a patient is asked to think of words that start with a certain letter.

posttraumatic amnesia (PTA): Memory loss that occurs after an injury to the head or brain.

procedural memory: See *implicit memory.*

psychogenic amnesia: Memory loss brought on by an emotionally stressful or overwhelming event.

retrograde amnesia: Loss of some or all memories from before the onset of amnesia.

seizure: A change in or a loss of consciousness, sometimes paired with convulsions, brought on by abnormal electrical activity in the brain.

short-term memory: Memory that is erased within thirty minutes.

stroke: A brain-damaging event caused by a clot in a blood vessel and often resulting in a range of symptoms that can include memory loss.

Stroop Color Word Interference Test: A test used to evaluate brain function in which a patient is asked to name one color when looking at the name of a different color.

synapse: The gap between nerve cells, where an electrical impulse passes from one cell to the other.

temporal lobe: A lobe in each hemisphere of the brain, responsible for processing sounds.

thiamine: Vitamin B1.

transient global amnesia: A short period of memory loss, with no obvious cause, that lasts a few hours.

traumatic brain injury: An injury to the brain resulting from an accident involving the head.

Wernicke-Korsakoff syndrome: Behavior changes and severe memory loss caused by vitamin deficiency and usually brought on by chronic alcohol abuse.

West Nile virus: A virus, spread by mosquitoes, that in some people leads to brain swelling that can cause amnesia.

Wisconsin Card Sorting Test (WCST): A test used to evaluate brain function in which a patient is asked to sort cards based on hints from the test-giver.

X-ray: A picture of the body that uses radiation to make an image of structures under the skin.

Organizations to Contact

Brain Injury Association of America (BIAA)

1608 Spring Hill Road, Suite 110
Vienna, VA 22182
Phone: (703) 761-0750
Information Hotline: (800) 444-6443
Fax: (703) 761-0755
www.biausa.org

The Brain Injury Association of America is the leading national organization for people affected by a life-altering traumatic brain injury. The organization provides support to the 5.3 million Americans living with such an injury.

National Institute of Neurological Disorders and Stroke (NINDS)

PO Box 5801
Bethesda, MD 20824
Phone: (800) 352-9424
www.ninds.nih.gov

A division of the National Institutes of Health, the National Institute of Neurological Disorders and Stroke provides the latest research and information on a variety of disorders of the brain and nervous system.

On With Life

715 S.W. Ankeny Road
Ankeny, IA 50023
Phone: (515) 965-1339
www.onwithlife.net

On With Life is a nonprofit organization that provides rehabilitation services and information for survivors of traumatic brain injuries.

Society for Neuroscience

1121 14th Street, Suite 1010
Washington, DC 20005
Phone: (202) 962-4000
Fax: (202) 962-4941
www.sfn.org

The Society for Neuroscience is a nonprofit organization of scientists and doctors who study the nervous system. It provides information on disorders of the brain and nervous system for doctors, scientists, and the general public.

ThinkFirst National Injury Prevention Foundation

29W120 Butterfield Road, Suite 105
Warrenville, IL 60555
Phone: (800) 844-6556
Fax: (630) 393-1402
www.thinkfirst.org

Formed by neurosurgeons frustrated at not being able to cure brain and spine injuries, the ThinkFirst National Injury Prevention Foundation focuses on educating the public about prevention and safety. It offers safety tips, information, videos, and other resources.

For Further Reading

Books

Arthur Bard and Mitchell Bard, *The Complete Idiot's Guide to Understanding the Brain*. Indianapolis, IN, Alpha, 2002. Brain anatomy, memory studies, and memory loss are among the topics covered in this book about the brain.

Russell Kahn, *How to Remember Everything: Grades 9–12: 183 Memory Tricks to Help You Study Better*. New York, Princeton Review, 2006. This book teaches memory tricks for learning large amounts of information quickly and holding on to it for years.

Elaine Landau, *Head and Brain Injuries*. Berkeley Heights, NJ, Enslow, 2002. Various types of head and brain injuries and their effects on health are discussed, along with treatments, recovery, and rehabilitation.

Diane Swanson, *Hmm?: The Most Interesting Book You'll Ever Read About Memory*. Tonawanda, NY, Kids Can Press, 2001. This book explains what memories are and how they are stored and triggered, and describes fun things to do with them. Part of the Mysterious You series.

Internet Sources

Eric H. Chudler, "A Computer in Your Head?" *ODYSSEY*, March 2001, http://faculty.washington.edu/chudler/computer.html.

Joshua Foer, "Remember This," *National Geographic*, November 2007, http://ngm.nationalgeographic.com/ngm/2007-11/memory/foer-text.html.

Jan Goodwin, "Forget Me Not," *Readers Digest*, June 2006, www.rd.com/stories/inspiration/amnesia-story/article.html.

Emily Sohn, "Memory by Hypnosis," *Science News for Kids*, January 16, 2008, www.sciencenewsforkids.org/articles/20080116/Note3.asp.

Videos

BrainWorks. Seattle, University of Washington Television, April 13, 2006, www.uwtv.org/programs/displayevent.aspx?rID=4909&fID=497.

Unknown White Male: A True Story. New York, Wellspring Media, 2005.

Web Sites

BrainConnection.com (www.brainconnection.com). Find articles, brain facts, memory games, and more at this Web site from Scientific Learning.

Neuroscience For Kids (http://faculty.washington.edu/chudler/neurok.html). Sponsored by the University of Washington, this Web site has experiments, activities, games, and articles to explain the workings of the brain and nervous system.

PBS Online (www.pbs.org/wgbh/nova/everest/exposure/stroopintro.html). This Web page gives an interactive demonstration of the Stroop test that climbers of Mount Everest take on their way to the summit to measure their mental abilities. (A similar test is used on many patients who have amnesia.)

Index

Picture Credits

Cover: Image copyright Hannamariah/Barbara Helgason, 2008. Used under license from Shutterstock.com.
AJPhoto/Photo Researchers, Inc., 67
AP Images, 50, 75
Image copyright William Casey, 2008. Used under license from Shutterstock.com, 49
© Walt Disney/courtesy Everett Collection, 82
Jim Dowdalls/Photo Researchers, Inc., 23
Image copyright Erni, 2008. Used under license from Shutterstock.com, 52
Frans Hals/The Bridgeman Art Library/Getty Images, 17
Image Source/Jupiterimages, 65
iStockPhoto.com/Eduardo Jose Bernardino, 29
iStockPhoto.com/Arthur Kwiatkowski, 31
iStockPhoto.com/Brandon Laufenberg, 14
iStockPhoto.com/photoGartner, 33
iStockPhoto.com/Gary Unwin, 42
iStockPhoto.com/Sean Warren, 36
iStockPhoto.com/Vasiliy Yakobchuk, 20
Image copyright Brian A. Jackson, 2008. Used under license from Shutterstock.com, 58
© 2008/Jupiterimages, 11
Image copyright Evgeny V. Kan, 2008. Used under license from Shutterstock.com, 81
Will & Deni McIntyre/Photo Researchers, Inc., 78
Image copyright Monkey Business Images, 2008. Used under license from Shutterstock.com, 76
Alfred Pasieka/Photo Researchers, Inc., 45
Phanie/Photo Researchers, Inc., 40
Purestock/Getty Images, 18
Francoise Sauze/Photo Researchers, Inc., 73
Frank Siteman/Doctor Stock/Science Faction/Getty Images, 70
© Ted Streshinsky/Corbis, 62
Zephyr/Photo Researchers, Inc., 47
Image copyright ZTS, 2008. Used under license from Shutterstock.com, 63

About the Author

Jenny MacKay is a copy editor for scientific and medical journals. She lives with her husband and two children in Sparks, Nevada, and is the author of *Fingerprinting*, *Criminal Profiling*, and *Phobias*.